Revitalizing
Practice

PETER LANG
New York • Washington, D.C./Baltimore • Bern
Frankfurt am Main • Berlin • Brussels • Vienna • Oxford

Revitalizing Practice

Collaborative Models for Theological Faculties

Edited by
Malcolm L. Warford

THE CONTRIBUTORS
Joseph A. Bessler
Peter T. Cha
Mary E. Hess
Timothy C. Tennent

PETER LANG
New York • Washington, D.C./Baltimore • Bern
Frankfurt am Main • Berlin • Brussels • Vienna • Oxford

Library of Congress Cataloging-in-Publication Data

Revitalizing practice: collaborative models
for theological faculties / edited by Malcolm L. Warford.
p. cm.
Includes bibliographical references and index.
1. Theological seminaries. I. Warford, Malcolm L.
BV4020.R48   230.071'1—dc22   2008031340
ISBN 978-1-4331-0225-7

Bibliographic information published by **Die Deutsche Bibliothek**.
Die Deutsche Bibliothek lists this publication in the "Deutsche
Nationalbibliografie"; detailed bibliographic data is available
on the Internet at http://dnb.ddb.de/.

Cover image: Adolph Gottlieb, *Dialogue I,* 1960, oil on canvas,
Albright-Knox Art Gallery, Buffalo, New York.
Gift of Seymour H. Knox, Jr., 1961

The paper in this book meets the guidelines for permanence and durability
of the Committee on Production Guidelines for Book Longevity
of the Council of Library Resources.

© 2008 Peter Lang Publishing, Inc., New York
29 Broadway, 18th floor, New York, NY 10006
www.peterlang.com

Printed in the United States of America

Contents

Preface

A few years ago, I was walking through the Albright-Knox Art Gallery in Buffalo, New York, and I happened into a room that contained a painting by Adolph Gottlieb called *Dialogue I.* (See book cover.) Suddenly I had before me a painting that seemed to represent artistically much of what we deal with in the practices of theological teaching and learning. If the painting represents, as the title suggests, an artistic conception of communication, then the two spheres seemed to me to represent a teacher and student or any two people or departments who converse within the formally intended practices of teaching and learning. I then interpreted the gray field in the background as the context of the constituent institutions and society in which this conversation occurs. The field seems neutral, but it consists, in fact, of subtle variations of texture, and like so much of what we take for granted in the world around us, the elements of this field are noticed typically in only a cursory way even as we weave and reweave the fabric of our common life. Finally, the dark, chaotic markings in the lower quadrant of the painting represent the tangled and less than logical reality of personal, emotional, and social dynamics that create the seldom acknowledged subtext for every human communication, no matter the formal structure and intent. Thus, the supposedly orderly practice of teaching and learning is actually filled with an immense complexity from which we can never escape. The educational question, therefore, is, how do we engage such complexity?

When faculty are asked to talk about their work, they often express a feeling of being overworked, but when that feeling is examined more closely, what becomes apparent is not that the volume of work has increased so much as that the diversity of the work has multiplied exponentially. Theological educators have to do more than one thing at a time, and they have to do it within a complicated institutional setting, and the only way they can be brought into the deepest practices of teaching and learning is to engage the full complexity of the institution's life.

During the last ten years, I have led The Lexington Seminar, a Lilly Endowment supported project on theological teaching and learning, which at its completion has involved more than forty-four seminaries and university divinity schools. Through this project, my colleagues and I have learned a number of things about institutions as well as the nature of theological education. We have learned that seminaries face a common set of challenges, especially issues of diversity, formation, institutional identity, and assessment. We have also learned that these are not technical problems but are instead the very stuff out of which teaching and learning are practiced. Yet faculties invariably find these issues of theological teaching and learning tantalizingly difficult to engage. Why? Because engaging such issues in a fruitful fashion requires an intentional setting and intentional strategies. The reality, though, is that, the settings in which these issues are usually engaged are decidedly not intentional. Typically, they consist of happenstance gatherings at someone's office door, casual conversations over lunch, or faculty meetings during which much other business must be discussed and little time is allotted to reflect deliberately on questions of teaching and learning. Such discussions frequently raise great interest, because the issues noted are quickly identified as crucial to the faculty, the students, and the institution. It is even agreed, frequently, that time should be set aside to deal with these issues. Seldom, however, is such time set aside, and so the issues remain unaddressed, the list of issues grows, and eventually, for many seminaries, the issues devolve into crises that threaten to overwhelm the institution.

The intention of The Lexington Seminar has been to establish a setting for conversation about issues of theological teaching and learning and to examine the stories in which each school, as a unique community, has woven its issues and its perceptions of itself. Out of this setting, through these conversations, and in the interpretation of the schools' narratives, the aim has been to support faculties in creating and implementing collaborative projects that engage the issues they have identified. These four elements—setting, conversation, narrative, and project—have been the key to the process of The Lexington Seminar.

The title of this book, *Revitalizing Practice*, is a phrase that points to the philosophical and educational writings of William James who never shies from the tougher questions and always urges us to move beyond the polite conversations of the seminar table to the grittier issues of what we are actually doing. The fact is that sometimes we are not doing much at all except continuing in diluted forms the patterns we have inherited. Unfortunately, as ecclesial structures continue to erode and funding sources become more difficult to find, seminaries—particularly small, denominational seminaries—cannot afford to continue such inherited patterns. Although some seminaries have the good fortune of affluence, proximity to major population centers, or connection with relatively healthy denominations and congregations, the typical denominational seminary struggles to reinvent itself and maintain some sense of equilibrium. In this context, strengthening the actual quality of education often seems a distant goal, deferred by the push of immediate pressures to balance the budget, patch up yet another constituent squabble, or go once more into the breach, searching for new programs to increase enrollment and revenue.

At the same time, university divinity schools face complicated issues around their own identity. Caught between the pluralistic world of the university and the more singular commitments of ecclesial traditions, theological faculties are brought into issues of differentiation and accountability that are particularly pressing in the specific question of how ministerial programs are situated in competing ideological and academic contexts. How to be true to these multiple realities and at the same time equip men and women for ministry in distinctive religious communities is a pressing concern. University divinity schools are gifted by growing fiscal resources that are in sharp contrast to the diminishing resources of denominational seminaries, but these resources alone will not solve the complicated educational and institutional questions university divinity schools face and how they can evoke new patterns for faculty to engage with these questions.

Throughout The Lexington Seminar, we have tried to offer a way of revitalizing practices of theological teaching and learning that offer hope for what lies ahead. Our assumption has been that theological faculties have the resourcefulness to deal with the issues they face. The challenge is to find the best means by which faculty colleagues can work together on these issues, not simply to understand them but to initiate activities that transform them.

Within this context, The Lexington Seminar in 2005 invited four faculty to join us in a mentor project on academic leadership. The aim was to have these theological teachers work alongside us in the planning and development of Seminar events even as they pursued their own research and thinking about key issues in theological education. We launched this inquiry with the clear goal of developing collaborative models for faculties that engage the thorny and complicated issues we face.

These collected essays express this common work. Each of the four chapters identifies a key issue, looks at its various dimensions, analyzes how the issue has been dealt with by schools participating in The Lexington Seminar, and, most importantly, offers a faculty collaborative model that faculties can adapt to their own situations and implement to engage the issue.

Joseph A. Bessler, the Robert Travis Peake Associate Professor of Theology at Phillips Theological Seminary, begins with an intriguing discussion of the habitat of theological seminaries and offers a model designed to encourage faculties to go outside their own experience and assumptions to see how many of their issues are shared by institutions beyond theological education. This kind of crossover experience permits faculty to see their situation anew and to learn from colleagues in similar but different settings.

Peter T. Cha, Associate Professor of Pastoral Theology at Trinity Evangelical Divinity School, pulls us into the complex world of institutional diversity and the changing character of the students we teach. Drawing on current explorations of theatrical improvisation for institutional learning, he invites us to explore the possibilities of improvisation as a way of learning together. He urges us to try on different perspectives and inhabit the diverse worlds of our students and colleagues.

Mary E. Hess, Associate Professor of Educational Leadership at Luther Seminary, explores how faculty colleagues can learn to listen and talk with each other at levels of insight and understanding not possible in the facile and more predictable discussions we usually have in our everyday lives. She suggests a process of appreciative listening that offers faculty a chance to learn together about themselves, the institutions they serve, and the students and communities that are at the center of their vocation as teachers in the church and academy.

Timothy C. Tennent, Professor of World Missions and Indian Studies at Gordon-Conwell Theological Seminary, raises the importance of global awareness for the ministry of the church and for the practices of theological teaching and learning. He invites us into a world café where reaching out to graduates actively engaged in ministries throughout the globe offers us the chance to learn from their experience and understand the implications for seminary teaching and programs.

Most of all, these four models for faculty engagement with issues of theological teaching and learning for the church's ministries provide settings and means that can be adapted in various ways for different faculties and institutions. Based on our assumption that faculty already have the creative resources to engage the issues they face, what we have tried to provide here are some settings and procedures that may help them call upon the practical wisdom they already possess.

Mac Warford

Acknowledgments

Books such as this come about because of the efforts of numerous talented people and invaluable institutions. Therefore, I cannot conclude without indicating my warm appreciation not only for those who have helped create this book but those who have been a part of The Lexington Seminar, which has proven to be a remarkable experience for all of us who have been privileged to lead this project over the years. In particular, it is important to recognize the contributions of Diamond Cephus, Jr., Victor Klimoski, Garth Rosell, Mary-Ann Winkelmes, and Gretchen Ziegenhals who have been the core community of leadership. At the same time, we have benefitted significantly from the participation of Raymond Williams in all of the June Seminars.

Specifically in regard to the Mentor Project in Academic Leadership, I want to mention Jane Gentry Vance, Martha Horne, Leland Eliason, and John Peter Kenney, who participated in the January Mentor Project Colloquia, and Don Pittman, Tite Tiénou, Barry Corey, Alice Mathews, Tim McFadden, Nick Nissley, and Jeanne McLean who provided valuable counsel to the mentor project participants.

I am indebted especially to Ken Huggins for his editorial work in the writing of the essays and to Victor Klimoski for his assistance in the development of the four models.

In particular, I want to acknowledge that the painting on the front cover is Adolph Gottlieb's *Dialogue I,* 1960, oil on canvas, 66×132" (167.64×335.28 cm) and is courtesy of Albright-Knox Art Gallery, Buffalo, New York; gift of Seymour H. Knox, Jr., 1961. Likewise, I want to acknowledge Stephen C. Rowe for his reference to William James's work as focused on "revitalizing practice" in his book *The Vision of William James* (Rockport, MA: Element Books Ltd., 1996), 16–17. The photograph on the back cover is courtesy of Jay Blossom, *In Trust* magazine. Design work for the figures in the book was provided by Mary Kulp, Graphics Insight, Harrisonburg, Virginia.

None of this would have been possible without the support and encouragement of Craig Dykstra and John Wimmer who have shepherded the religion programs of Lilly Endowment Inc. for so many years. In the beginning, of course, was the invitation by Fred Hofheinz to take up this project and create this program in theological teaching for the church's ministries. I am also grateful to Lexington Theological Seminary for its hospitality as the supporting institution for The Lexington Seminar. Finally, The Lexington Seminar could not have achieved any of its stated goals without the enthusiastic participation of the seminaries and divinity schools listed at the back of this book.

Mac Warford

1. *Seminaries as Endangered Habitats in a Fragile Ecosystem: A New Ecology Model*

Joseph A. Bessler

In the fall of 1997, a special committee appointed by the board of trustees of Phillips Theological Seminary recommended that the school move from its historical location in Enid, Oklahoma, to the larger metropolitan area of Tulsa, where the seminary had been operating a satellite campus since 1986. Facing significant deficits in the early to mid-1990s, compounded by the costs of maintaining two campuses, the board agreed. By 1999, the school had received not only property but a modern corporate complex to redesign for seminary education. With strong support from the board and key donors, the seminary began to build the fiscal strength of the seminary. Campus renovations were completed in time for the beginning of the fall 2003 semester. A six-year process, the wholesale transition from one physical location to another, capped an even longer struggle for institutional survival.

Due to financial stresses in the mid-1990s, several faculty and staff members were let go, and several others who had retired were not replaced. At the same time, full-time faculty members offered introductory courses at churches in Oklahoma City, Oklahoma; Springfield, Missouri; Wichita, Kansas; and Bentonville, Arkansas, to help recruit students. The faculties of the Enid and Tulsa campuses also regularly made the hourlong drive to meet halfway at First Christian Church in Stillwater, Oklahoma, for joint faculty senate and committee meetings. At the same time, the institution sought to strengthen its relationships with non-Disciple judicatories and reached out as well to African American, Native American, and Hispanic communities in the form of special scholarships, new master's programs, and hiring initiatives.

In the mid- to late 1990s, PTS applied for and received two Lilly Endowment grants—a capacity-building grant and an educational technology grant—which the school used in its redesign of the new building and its work with faculty on teaching with technology. An institutional self-study, completed in 1999, expressed the renewed confidence of the institution; it had weathered serious challenges and was now on the right path. That judgment has been solidly confirmed in recent years. Yet, despite an increase in endowment from a little over $3 million in 1997 to over $14 million in 2007, the institution still struggles annually to fund the programs currently in place.[1]

The Changing Context of Theological Education

The experience of this one, medium-sized Christian church (Disciples of Christ) seminary is hardly unique. While a geographical move of the main campus to ensure survival remains atypical, the health of many small to medium-sized denominational Protestant seminaries has shifted dramatically from a state of flourishing in the 1950s to a struggle for survival in recent decades (Chaves 1999, 180–181).[2] The decline has dramatically impacted the work of all the institutional players at these schools: the boards of trustees, the presidents, the deans, and the faculties. Many schools—including some that appear to be doing well—face challenges that call for what Ronald Heifetz (1994, 8) describes as adaptive change—that is, a process of change requiring innovation and learning and not simply the kind of technical changes that institutions deploy when facing routine problems.

In the 1950s, congregations, church-related colleges, denominational bodies, seminaries, and faculty-producing divinity schools thrived in a mutually supportive system of ecclesial and academic life. In broad strokes, here is how that system worked: The cultural dominance and prestige of mainline Protestant denominations throughout much of twentieth-century America ensured that colleges had a steady stream of young white male students. Upon graduation these young men then entered denominational seminaries or university divinity schools. Following the lead of the university divinity schools, many denominational seminaries stressed the importance of equipping each student to become the scholar-preacher that was deemed then the model for congregational ministry.

Stresses upon what seemed to be a cooperative system of mainline denominations, church-related colleges, denominational seminaries, and university-related divinity schools began with the decline of church attendance in the mid-1960s and the loss of much of the baby-boom generation over subsequent decades. A decline in the cultural status of ministers accompanied these losses, which fueled, in time, a significant decrease in young white males pursuing careers in ministry as they graduated from college religion departments and humanities programs. In addition, with an increasing number of mixed-denominational marriages, churchgoers themselves began to take a more consumer-oriented approach to religion, frequently shopping for a church home that would meet the needs of both spouses and their children. These and other forces resulted in sharp and continuing decreases in the funding of the denominational structures that had so consistently funded denominational seminaries. About this situation Gary Peluso-Verdend and Jack Seymour (2005) write: "The ecology of institutions that previously recruited for ministry and supported congregations...has almost dissipated" (58).

Recent Experiments in Theological Education

From the mid- to late 1960s and 1970s forward, one sees denominational seminaries adopting various strategies to secure two ingredients crucial for their survival: (1) adequate financial resources and (2) an adequate applicant pool.[3] A quick review of some of these institutional strategies from the 1970s, 1980s, and 1990s shows that schools have demonstrated genuine creativity in their attempts to cope with these emerging problems.

Instead of the process of pastoral formation for a relatively homoge-neous student body that one saw in the denominationally stable 1950s, one finds from the 1970s forward a pattern of institutions seeking to expand the diversity of their applicant pool. This shift in recruitment strategy ran parallel to the diminishing financial support coming to seminaries from denominational bodies and the subsequently increased financial burden that seminaries had to shoulder alone. As many seminaries found themselves more precariously freestanding than ever before, they needed new theologically informed visions to help guide their search for new applicants and sources of revenue. In the 1970s, for example, and motivated by the theological vision of ecumenism—generated in part by the energy of Vatican II and the continuing influence of Protestant commitments to cooperation—many seminaries expanded not only the denominational diversity of their faculties but that of their student-applicant pools as well. Moreover, the theological school consor-tium movement enabled ecumenical and institutional cooperation among a range of competing urban schools, creating a further impetus toward theological diversity while also consolidating curricular standards across denominational lines.[4]

The new emphasis on ecumenism and Christian cooperation among churches, however, did not stem the tide of individuals either leaving main-line religious communities altogether or reducing their level of actual and financial participation. In fact, at one level, ecumenism may have fueled the secularizing impulse by suggesting that religious particularity within the

Christian fold no longer mattered, giving rise to a more consumer-oriented approach to church shopping.

If for many denominational seminaries in the 1970s the idealism of the ecumenical movement coincided with their institutional attempts to broaden their bases of financial support and student applications, the 1980s saw the rise of a counterstrategy. Concerned that mainline denominations were exchanging their traditional theological identities for a kind of watered-down ecumenism and liberal identification with culture, this approach argued that denominations and denominational seminaries needed to maintain their distinctive theological identities in order to survive and grow. While often guided by explicitly theological movements, in what emerged as postliberal theology, these new strategies were also deeply influenced by a market logic of competition designed to stem the hemorrhaging of denominations.[5]

The sails of the open-house experimentation of the 1970s were trimmed but not reversed in the mid-1980s and 1990s by denominational concerns related to maintaining distinctive public identities.[6] Experimentation to increase student enrollment, especially nontraditional students, continued in the 1980s and 1990s, with institutions offering new degree programs, block scheduling, off-campus courses, multiple campus sites, and online courses to attract new students. Increasingly, however, emphases on denominational identity could not reverse the institutional needs of seminaries for a broader pool of applicants.[7] By the late 1990s, the need for financial resources and students contributed to increased competition within denominational school networks—bending, if not breaking, historically established geographical-comity arrangements.

Squeezing the Middle

While Protestant denominational seminaries were caught up in interdenominational and intratheological disputes, a variety of multidenominational schools committed to traditions of biblical and theological orthodoxy experienced real success by combining market realism with the affirmation of long-standing Christian traditions. Schools such as Fuller, Gordon-Conwell, Bethel, and Asbury established virtually national, brand-name recognition through their alignment with the growing evangelical movement, new long-distance campus arrangements, and online curricula. In contrast to the faltering more liberal tradition, the evangelical movement has nurtured the contours of a relatively stable theological ecosystem. While not all evangelicals are convinced that the evangelical movement's rise to cultural prominence is an unalloyed blessing, there is no denying that evangelical institutional and educational strategies will continue to influence the practice of theological education in the decades ahead.

One striking aspect of the overall evangelical movement has been its creative use of technology. Evangelical seminaries have used their technological and media savvy to bolster their own capacities for institutional outreach to congregations, publishing houses, and parachurch organizations. The rise of megachurches, with their heavy investments in technology, Christian youth programming, and dramatic preaching, has furthered the development of a growing ecclesial-seminary partnership in evangelical circles.[8] While more liberal critics have frequently viewed evangelical institutions as following too closely an American consumerist orientation, the critics are also now paying attention to evangelical successes in technological and organizational areas to see how they might reimagine their own institutional structures to be similarly adaptive.

If multicampus evangelical megaschools are pressuring small to medium-sized denominational seminaries from the conservative side, absorbing dollars and students by creatively forming new educational habitats, the major, brand-name divinity schools, such as Yale, Harvard, Duke, Princeton, Vanderbilt, Emory, and Chicago, are pressuring seminaries from the liberal, academic side. Aided in fund raising by their close ties to major universities, these divinity schools have continued to recruit the best-prepared college graduates, many of whom now come straight out of college. Younger students, who once would first have attended their denominational seminary before attending a university-related divinity school for doctoral study, are now pursuing their master's-level work at the divinity schools.[9] Denominational seminaries without national brand-name recognition find themselves struggling to establish a sustainable habitat of students and financial resources.

Baumol's Cost Disease: When Even More Is Not Keeping Up

Sociologist Mark Chaves (2006) has recently suggested a possible explanation for the thirty-five-year trend toward larger congregations that may help shed light on the situation facing denominational seminaries: the economic concept called Baumol's cost disease.[10] First developed in the mid-1960s by economists William J. Baumol and William G. Bowen, the concept of Baumol's cost disease sought to make sense of financial-stability concerns arising in the not-for-profit business sector. "The basic idea," says Chaves, "is simple: if there is increasing productivity and efficiency in some sectors of the economy, and if wages increase in those sectors, then wages also will increase in other sectors, or else talent will move to the sectors in which wages are increasing" (23–24).

Because, with few exceptions, pastors' wages, from the 1970s forward, did not keep pace with rising increases in other professions, those professions rather quickly eclipsed the ministry both in salary and prestige. Ministerial talent went elsewhere. Chaves continues, focusing on the question of efficiency:

> Some kinds of activities cannot be made more efficient. It probably takes about as much preparation and effort to produce *Hamlet* or perform a Beethoven symphony in the 21st century as it did centuries ago. Activities that have at their core human effort, training, practice, attention and presence cannot be made much more efficient. No technological invention or social innovation makes it possible to reduce the level of input into such activities and still get the same level of output, so enterprises organized around such activities cannot be made more efficient without a reduction in quality.
>
> Churches are subject to Baumol's cost disease. Like schools, universities, theater companies and symphony orchestras, churches face ever-rising real costs with no significant opportunities to reduce those costs by becoming more efficient. The only options in such a situation are to sacrifice quality or increase revenue. (23–24)

In the face of dwindling denominations, the search for new financial resources, and an expanding student-applicant pool, theological schools have begun to resemble not-for-profit businesses.[11] While Anthony Ruger (1999) is right in saying that many schools have improved their financial situation over the past twenty years—in the 1980s due to the stock market and in the 1990s due to individual contributions and corporate gifts—many of those same schools remain financially stressed. To have really benefited from the stock market in the 1980s, schools needed an endowment to invest. While this point seems obvious, many ATS schools had little to no endowment. In fact, as of 2005–2006, the median amount of long-term investments of the 202 ATS schools that reported long-term investments was $11 million (Association of Theological Schools 2006).[12] But that median number does not adequately demonstrate the vast difference between the wealthy schools and the rest. Eighty percent of the reporting schools (approximately 160 of them) have at most $29 million in long-term investments. The remaining 20 percent (or 40 schools) have a median of $74 million, which extends from Princeton's transcendent $860 million to the Earlham School of Religion's $33 million.

While many schools, including Phillips, have benefited significantly from the 1990s trend identified by Ruger, namely individual contributions and corporate grants, such gifts have not ensured continued growth. Rising health-care costs, rising building- maintenance costs, rising energy costs, rising costs to keep pace with educational technologies (especially those that enable schools to reach more students), rising costs of admissions, and the rising costs of keeping pace with ATS and other accrediting-body initiatives on globalization programs, institutional assessment, faculty diversification initiatives, and so on, threaten to erase or minimize the gains many schools thought they had achieved. Not only are costs rising, but the rise has become especially steep for schools with little endowment income. In order to cope, many seminaries are faced with an ever-expanding annual budget, which requires increases in tuition. Such high costs make it difficult for schools—even ones experiencing real generosity—to feel that they are getting ahead financially.

The growing wealth gap in theological education deserves urgent and serious attention. The figures cited above point to a deepening crisis in which the stock market gains of the major divinity schools in the 1980s and their greater access to individual and corporate gifts in the 1990s have so outpaced the growth of small to medium-sized denominational schools that any sense of institutional parity or sense of contribution to a common vocation is becoming untenable.[13]

Chaves's (2006) use of Baumol's cost-disease analysis deserves closer attention as seminaries seek new ways of thriving programmatically and financially. If Chaves is right about a continuing trend toward larger congregations across denominations, then one can expect that the continued financial stress on smaller congregations will lead to fewer congregations being able to hire M.Div.-educated pastors (who are now frequently middle-aged, with family, looking for health-care benefits and a salary package able to cope with their indebtedness, increasingly complicated by student loans and credit-card debt built up during their seminary years). These tendencies will pressure ministerial candidates to seek shorter ministry-degree programs as well as the best financial-aid packages to minimize the costs of time and treasure in seminary.[14] Even as denominations seek to reverse the trend of smaller, dying congregations by investing in the development of new congregations in growing population centers, denominations and seminaries both face uphill battles.

As seminaries have sought to increase revenue to stave off the effects of Baumol's cost disease, they have begun to reach out to new, nontraditional students (from differing denominational and ethnic backgrounds) and to new individual and corporate funding sources. In "Financing Protestant Theological Schools," Anthony Ruger (1999) writes that "overall, gifts and grants are the single largest source of revenue for theological schools from 1971 to 1991" (115). While noting significant differences among the nine Protestant denominations studied, he claims that "the real story about gifts and grants...concerns the shift away from denominational sources of support" (115). The shift away from *denominational* sources of support, however, requires a further asterisk insofar as most individuals making significant personal contributions to seminaries, and influencing corporate gifts, tend to be persons both formed by and rooted in congregations.

Renewing the Congregational Connection

Declines in denominational funding have dramatically increased the importance of congregational support as an essential lifeline in the seminary's new marketplace habitat. Not all congregations, of course, have thrived, and among those that have, not all are convinced that seminaries are committed to educating effective leaders for ministry. Faced with congregational, and sometimes denominational, calls for alternative routes to ordination that bypass the traditional school model, denominational seminaries are increasingly challenged to win back the support of a constituency they took for granted during the heyday of denominational giving: congregations.

Gary Peluso-Verdend and Jack Seymour (2005), in summarizing their conclusions from a four-year experiment at Garrett-Evangelical Seminary to build stronger connections to congregations, insist that establishing a life-sustaining ecology based on developing leaders for congregational ministry requires of theological institutions "trust and collegiality among the seminary, its closest judicatories, its faculty, and local congregations" (59). They go on, however—with italics for emphasis—to underscore a key obstacle to such institutional cooperation.

> *However, how this* [relationship between seminary and congregation] *occurs and how this becomes the focus of an institutional mission when faculty guilds often divide and focus faculty work in individualistic patterns are crucial issues....*(59)

While the habits of faculty culture represent a central and vital asset to theological education, Peluso-Verdend and Seymour argue that faculty guilds also represent an important obstacle to adaptive change.

Barriers in Faculty Culture

If denominational seminaries in this new situation are analogous to not-for-profit businesses, then sustaining a healthy habitat requires them to make serious and significant choices about their institutional attachments. Increasingly funded by individuals and corporate grants and less so by their denominational bodies, many seminaries need to align themselves more closely to traditional denominational identities and congregations on the one hand, while casting a wider net of engagement with secular culture and nontraditional audiences of theological education on the other. Not an easy task.

The multiple directions in which institutions are pulled for resources and students has placed significant stress on the presidents and deans of denominational seminaries, as well as on the faculties, to make significant adaptive changes. Unfortunately, the vast majority of presidents, deans, and faculty members have not been professionally prepared to lead theological schools in a not-for-profit business context. Formed instead by the powerful ethos of the academy with its commitments to scholarship and disciplinary focus, these institutional leaders tend to be poorly equipped for making the kinds of judgments now demanded of them.[15]

In a 1997 essay, "Why Seminaries Don't Change: A Reflection on Faculty Specialization," Edward Farley observes that despite fifteen years of intense inquiry of theological education, "little or no reform has taken place in either seminary or graduate degree programs" (135). The core reason behind institutional resistance to change, argues Farley, is the professional formation of faculty:

> Because the faculty has an almost exclusive role in determining the content and standards for the degree programs, it tends to be the central source of a school's ethos and standards. To the extent that seminaries imitate what American higher education expects of faculty members, they will require that faculty members be scholar teachers within the parameters of a specialized field, such as social ethics, New Testament, or American religious history. Tenure and promotion depend on accomplishments within this specialized field. (135)

Moreover, the process of "specialization begins in graduate school, or even before" (135). And because "specialization sets the terms for a faculty member's participation in the life of a school, it is perhaps the most powerful structure at work in faculty life: the faculty member's existence and legitimation are at stake when his or her field is threatened" (137). Insofar as a curriculum consists of a collection of academic specializations, Farley claims that a kind of mutual agreement, a hands-off principle, exists among the competing disciplines. "A faculty member thus assures the continued existence of his own specialty by agreeing to protect the existence of others. Unfortunately, the hands-off agreement breeds a certain indifference to general concerns affecting the school's health" and prevents the faculty from "assisting with the nuts and bolts of institutional maintenance" (139). Thus, writes Farley, "it becomes difficult for faculty to participate in grand designs, theories of educational transformation or new pedagogical paradigms" (139).

While pessimistic about changing faculty culture, short of dire institutional challenges, Farley encourages attempts to help faculty talk across the specialization divide: "Faculty retreats can be useful if they allow small groups to tackle general issues....Whatever the methods used, schools need to create a faculty accustomed to transspecialty inquiry and discussion. Such a faculty is the necessary condition for genuine reform" (143).

While Farley sets out to explain "why *seminaries* don't change" (my emphasis), his analysis involves a central component of the broader ecosystem of theological education as a whole: the culture of faculty specialization.[16]

If faculty culture is the obstacle that Peluso-Verdend and Seymour and Farley believe it to be, then helping faculties talk about common issues across their specializations may be a key ingredient in helping seminaries engage in the kind of adaptive changes they are being pressed to make.

Lessons of The Lexington Seminar

It is one thing to say that seminary faculty members ought to learn to talk with one another beyond their specializations, or that seminary faculties must reach beyond their scholarly isolation and participate more fully in shaping the life of their institutions. It is quite another thing to try to help faculties engage in that broader praxis of institutional conversation. Since 1999, The Lexington Seminar has provided just such help to seminary administration and faculty members. Further, many of the narratives and projects developed by schools that have participated in the Seminar have identified issues of teaching and learning directly traceable to the continuing efforts of theological schools to create sustainable and growing habitats of adequate financial resources and potential students.[17]

That many schools and faculties, across geographical and denominational habitats, share similar frustrations with respect to resources and a potential student body, suggests that structural economic forces akin to Baumol's cost disease are at work in many theological schools. The narratives developed by Seminar schools frequently show faculty members frustrated not only by having to do *more* work with fewer resources but also by having to do *more adaptive* work—with an increasingly diverse and nontraditional student body—with little or no professional acknowledgment or reward to show for it. In a number of school narratives, for example, seminary faculty members wonder aloud whether they can recognize their own vocation as scholar-teachers anymore. In addition, behind the numerous narratives of student diversity lies faculty members' bewilderment about their own adequacy to reach, teach, and help the range of students in their care.

Taken as a whole, the narratives constitute a unique inside look at the kinds of felt pressure on theological-school faculties, deans, and presidents, who rarely discuss such core problems among themselves, let alone in conversation with other schools. Even assuming that the schools' narratives and reports attempt to put the best face on their efforts, these documents demonstrate a remarkable candor, revealing the felt texture of the difficulties faculties face when engaging in processes of adaptive change.

If the narratives provide rich descriptions of the kinds of pressures I have associated with the now-endangered habitats of many denominational schools and the corrosive forces of Baumol's cost disease, the project reports evidence a willingness to engage in processes of conversation that might change the specialization culture of seminary faculties. The project reports themselves, reflecting on the schools' three-year projects, note some basic but important learning across the spectrum of participating schools. A line from Claremont School of Theology's report (2000) can speak for many: "We have learned that a conversation that moves into the core of an organization's values and purpose takes a long time." McCormick Theological Seminary's report (2000) notes, "Time is needed for faculty to work on major issues." And the report of the Lutheran School of Theology at Chicago (1999) says, "There need to be conversations that are carried on without the pressure of immediate decision making." Others, like the Phillips report, note the consistent energy and attention that institutional change requires.

To help facilitate that quality of attention and conversation, a number of schools borrowed from The Lexington Seminar's residential retreat model and used some of their Lexington Seminar grant funds to take administrators and faculty (and spouses) to a setting in which carefully designed time and space make room for serious and sustained discussion of educational issues that matter.

While projects varied, one sees a consistent effort in the reports to connect with and listen to constituent groups that are not simply audiences but stakeholders in the newly emerging not-for-profit theological school. For example, Calvin Theological Seminary (1999) developed surveys for alumni/ae assessments of their education, Austin Presbyterian Theological Seminary (1999) instituted intentional conversations between faculty and trustees, and Virginia Theological Seminary (1999) sent faculty to theological institutions in the African, Central American, and Caribbean nations from which it draws its international students.

Although the project reports confirmed Farley's insight that members of specialized faculties rarely take time to talk with one another about things that matter, the reports also indicate that many faculties can be nudged into genuinely helpful conversations given time and a sense of leisure in which to connect with one another. As the Luther Seminary report (2001) puts it, "What we've discovered is that when we clear the space for conversations about teaching and learning, we're energized by it and know that it's valuable—so valuable that we have made plans for a number of additional, institutionally supported efforts to continue the conversation." The report of Eastern Baptist Theological Seminary (2000) concurs: "Putting things out on the table without seeking to resolve them immediately is a powerful means of building trust and respect. Hearing one another without anxiety and seeing attitudes change over a period of time generates internal confidence in our ability to get through resistance together."

If, as Heifetz (1994) suggests, the task of leadership is to help communities face the adaptive challenges confronting them, The Lexington Seminar has demonstrated the capacity and desire of theological faculties to engage in conversations that remind them of their high calling.

A New Paradigm for Faculty Identity

In light of Chaves's discussion of the emerging not-for-profit model of denominational school habitats, Anthony Tommasini's article in the *New York Times*, "Looking for Citizens for a Few Good Orchestras" (2006, 29), offers a plausible model for equipping faculties to deal with the changing landscape of theological education. As Chaves noted in his description of Baumol's cost disease, organizations such as orchestras and seminaries have limits on improving efficiency. Many local orchestras have been facing threats to their resources and audiences similar to those faced by denominational seminaries.

Tommasini focuses on the training of professional musicians as a resource for addressing "the decline of both music and music appreciation" that faces so many orchestras. If the current "situation is to change," he writes, "then an ability to connect with the public, to generate excitement and sympathy for classical music among young people and adult audiences, must become essential to the job description of every professional in the field" (29).

Tommasini's article opens with a description of the professional musician's formation that is eerily similar to Farley's description of faculty culture.

> Let's say that an orchestra has an opening for a violinist. The two finalists are both young men, both graduates of top conservatories. One is a brilliant player who has made several appearances as a soloist with noted orchestras. The other has been active in his home city playing in a contemporary music ensemble and teaching at the neighborhood music school. In concerts he has proven adept at giving informational talks before the performance of, say, a difficult new work.

> Which candidate will get the job? Typically, the audition committee and the orchestra's music director would choose the violinist with the impressive soloist credentials and the bravura technique....

> Too many orchestras, intent on recruiting the absolutely best players..., have tended to undervalue a musician's skills at outreach. (29)

Tommasini then goes on to describe a new program, called the Academy, developed by two elite institutions, Carnegie Hall and the Juilliard School, to challenge the virtuosic assumptions of the professional musical guild.

> Think of it. Through this program talented musicians on the brink of a career will be chosen as resident artists at Carnegie Hall and the Juilliard School...not because they have won fancy competitions or secured professional management, but because they are willing to work in public schools in New York. (29)

Tommasini reports a conversation with Joseph W. Polisi, president of Juilliard, in which the latter "envisioned an orchestra with such a vibrant presence in the community—with members so involved in teaching and taking music to schools and community centers—that 'citizens will feel it unthinkable that this ensemble would go out of business'" (29).

If the analogy of orchestras' circumstances with those of seminaries seems far-fetched, it shouldn't. Just when Protestant denominational theological schools are facing the need to be more publicly involved and visible, Elizabeth Lynn and Barbara G. Wheeler (1999), in a four-city study, report the bad news:

> Whatever the reasons, seminaries are not viewed as *civic* assets in their communities or beyond. They are not part of the civic mix. When important decisions about social policies or community projects are at stake, seminaries and those who work in them are rarely asked to participate, even to comment, except by the occasional religion reporter who needs a quotation on a religiously tinged issue. (5)

Put more strongly, "Whether or not this strategy [civic quietness] is intentional, it effectively characterizes the seminaries in each of the four cities we visited. Seminaries are quiet to the point of absence in their local communities" (1999, 7).

Creating a wider, more active role for seminaries in public life requires a quality of conversation in seminaries between administration and faculty about institutional identity rarely seen in recent decades. While there is no denying the current time of troubles for many seminaries trying to keep pace with rising costs and shrinking denominational contributions, there are signs of creative and courageous renewal. Given their radically changed circumstances, the seminaries that flourish will be the ones whose faculties are able to reach out to their constituents and become more involved with their communities.

Breaking Free of Old Habits

In light of the preceding analysis, it seems apparent that many a seminary's traditional reliance upon its denomination for adequate funding and a steady applicant pool has kept it from pursuing a more visible face and voice in the public realm. Further, the professional preparation of theological faculty at university divinity schools has also reinforced habits that encourage faculty members to view their responsibilities to the institution in the fairly narrow terms of contribution to their specialized disciplines. Current pressures on denominational seminaries to become more public, more closely linked both to congregations and to public commitments in the local community, however, are causing seminary faculties to reassess their professional identity, priorities, and directions of research.

As schools become increasingly aware of the ecological threats and possibilities within their religious and cultural settings, commitment to the "mission of the seminary" will increasingly be measured in terms of actual contribution to the kinds of teamwork necessary for seminary faculty members and administrators to renew the lives of these endangered schools. Not only in new ATS Standards, but throughout society at large, institutions are now expected to develop cultures of institutional assessment and improvement. Such expectations have created a "new" site for ongoing theological research, namely the theological school itself.

Leadership: It's Not Just for Presidents and Deans Anymore

Peter Senge, in an article on "The Leader's New Work: Building Learning Organizations," takes aim at our mythic assumptions of leaders as heroes (1990). Such myths, he argues, play to a preoccupation with "short-term results" instead of helping us focus on "systemic forces and collective learning" (8). We need, he says to reimagine leaders as "designers," as "teachers," and as "stewards" (9)—as figures who help shape, orient, and enable organizations to be not only adaptive but generative. In Senge's and others' new approaches to leadership, it is not only the model of leadership that is being reworked, but that of the organization as well.

In the old heroic model of leadership, institutions (such as towns, communities, families, and schools) functioned as fixed, stereotypically feminized objects of a hero's salvific activity—passive, helpless in the face of threatening forces, and in need of rescue. In more recent models, including Senge's, institutions are viewed as living organisms, situated within complex cultural geographies, and possessing vital capacities for adaptive and strategic change. Contemporary theorists, including Senge, have *spatialized* leadership—shifting away from earlier preoccupations with the kairotic timing of the hero's coming to an emphasis on the diverse roles and spaces from within which organizational leadership is exercised. Skilled leadership in the newer models, according to Senge, requires skills of designing, teaching, and stewarding that enable the inherent creativity and leadership within the organization to work cooperatively and cohesively.

In the body of this essay, I have used the language of ecology and habitat to help theological schools, and especially faculty members, recognize and accept their collective responsibility for shaping their institutions in ways that create new, life-sustaining habits of teaching and learning. The language of habitat is also useful for understanding what Senge calls the principle of "creative tension" (8). "Creative tension," says Senge, "comes from seeing where we want to be, our 'vision,' and telling the truth about where we are, our 'current reality'" (8). Unless we face the reality of our situation—where we are culturally and economically—vision will not be of any help.

Tommasini offers an illustration of the importance of recognizing "current reality" based on his study of local and regional orchestras. Orchestras, he notes, have begun to recognize their fragile economic predicament and know that if the "situation is to change, then an ability to connect with the public, to generate excitement and sympathy for classical music among young people and adult audiences, must become essential to the job description of every professional in the field" (29). Similarly, as many denominational schools realize that they must become more visible and involved in the community, faculty development must also be seen in the wider context of contributing to institutional stability and renewal.

Model for Faculty Development in the New Ecology of Cooperative Partnerships

In this portion of the essay I propose a three-day model (see Figure 1.1) that is not simply about faculty development but also about the dean's own development as a leader in Senge's model of designer, teacher, and steward. Senge summarizes the requisite tasks of those three titles respectively as "the ability to build shared vision, to bring to the surface and challenge prevailing mental models, and to foster more systemic patterns of thinking" (9). The model presented here attempts to tap into each of these three new tasks of leadership.

Preliminary Step: Planning and Preparing the Faculty

Permeating my project proposal is what Senge identified as the first task of the new leadership: building a shared vision. As seminary deans and presidents impress on their faculty colleagues the importance of the seminary claiming responsibility for its adaptive future, they must at the same time create a space of structured exploration for faculty members to come together and own the journey into what Winnicott refers to as the "potential space" of habitat renewal (Mendenhall and Ronsheim 2006, 110). Because such a period of structured exploration is itself a threshold into the potential space of the new habitat, presidents and deans will also need to prepare faculty for an ongoing conversation of institutional learning and change.

Figure 1.1: Three-Day Model for Faculty Development in the New Ecology of Cooperative Partnerships.

Goal: Enable faculty to perceive and adapt to the changing habitat of the seminary.

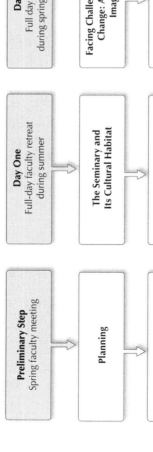

Preliminary Step
Spring faculty meeting

Planning

Dean prepares faculty for engaging process of institutional learning by offering questions to address, for example:

- What would it mean for us to think of our theological school as an organism in a habitat rather than as a machine that "turns out" graduates?

- How are organizations similar to ours coping with similar difficulties?

- What might it mean for us as an institution and faculty to engage with and expand our own institutional habitat?

Day One
Full-day faculty retreat during summer

The Seminary and Its Cultural Habitat

Faculty are asked to address the following concepts:

- Perceive their institutional setting not as a geographical point but as a life-sustaining habitat.

- Use the language of cultural geography to extend their analysis of their institutional habitat.

- Begin to look at their institution as existing within a habitat, considering its history, patterns of funding, applicant pool, strengths, fragility, and current needs.

Day Two
Full day off campus during spring or fall semester

Facing Challenges of Adaptive Change: An Analogical Imagination

Have faculty visit a selected institution analogous with their own and spend the day with the personnel of that institution. This should allow faculty to do the following:

- Attend to the vocation at the heart of the visited institution.

- Ask the institution's staff and director about its own structural and audience problems.

- Perceive how the institution is reimagining its work and audience.

- Ask individual personnel how addressing these issues has changed their perceptions of their vocations.

Day Three
Full day during the same semester as Day Two

Reimagining Our Internal and Public Commitments

Dean asks faculty to address the need to expand and stabilize a life-sustaining habitat.

- Naming the constituencies in the school's habitat/context.

- Being realistic about our obligations to those constituencies.

- Thinking theologically about
  ○ an ethos of faith and reason
  ○ stewardship as commitment to enhance school's public presence and voice
  ○ vocation as personal and as corporate calling

The three-day model proposed here is an initial exploratory process that will require a one-day faculty retreat during the summer and two full days of faculty colloquia in a single semester.[18] Working in conversation with key faculty members, the dean should have all basic arrangements for those three days—including reservations, special readings or assignments, and confirmations from presenters—already in place. The dean should use a portion of one of the spring semester faculty meetings to call the faculty to a sustained period of institutional learning. Reminding the faculty that such attention is necessary not only for reasons of institutional accreditation but for the sustained survival and success of the school itself, the dean should indicate the model's specific goals and the major elements of the plan itself.

Sharing an outline of the meetings proposed here, the dean should walk the faculty through appropriate details of the major steps in the process:

Day One: From Machine to Organism: The Seminary and Its Cultural Habitat

Day Two: Facing Challenges of Adaptive Change: An Analogical Imagination

Day Three: Reimagining Our Internal and Public Commitments

Demonstrating that the topics and agenda items have been developed in practical detail can help allay faculty anxieties about expectations and feasibility. The dean might also emphasize the restful, conversational setting selected for the faculty retreat, signaling the heightened quality of the anticipated conversation and its perceived worth to institutional leadership.[19] To add specificity to the goals of the retreat, the dean should suggest that the faculty anticipate several purposeful questions, such as the following:

- What would it mean for us to think of our theological school as an organism in a habitat rather than as a machine that "turns out" graduates?
- How are organizations similar to ours coping with similar difficulties?
- What might it mean for us as an institution and faculty to engage with and expand our own institutional habitat?

Finally, the dean should assign a text or other media assignment to help faculty prepare for the faculty retreat and the later two sessions, further demonstrating to faculty colleagues the care with which the program has been prepared. For Day One, the dean might advise faculty to read a chapter or two from an introductory text on cultural geography, such as Tim Cresswell's *Place: A Short Introduction* (2007). For Day Two, the dean might select an article or essay about creative responses from the arts community to economic and cultural pressures—perhaps a nontechnical essay about Baumol's work on the arts or education or the chapter on the intrinsic benefits of art from *Gifts of the Muse: Reframing the Debate about the Benefits of the Arts* (McCarthy et al. 2005). For Day Three, the dean might select a text that focuses on the vocation of the faculty member, such as John Bennett's *Academic Life: Hospitality, Ethics, and Spirituality* (2003).

Day One—From Machine to Organism: The Seminary and Its Cultural Habitat

The educational goal for the first day is to help faculty members absorb the implications of a metaphorical shift in the way that theological schools perceive themselves. That shift—as underscored by the ATS *Handbook of Accreditation* (2006, 43–44)—involves viewing the theological school not as a machine but as an organism that exists within a specific habitat and ecology, particularly with respect to its history, its organizational environment, and the vocation of the faculty members themselves. While this linguistic shift has become part of the evaluative discourse of theological institutions, there is little evidence that the metaphor and its implications for organizational life have become fully operational for most seminaries. Therefore, beginning the process of making this metaphor an essential part the faculty's perception of the school is a key purpose for this first meeting.

To unpack and elaborate on the implications of the organism metaphor, the dean might invite an outside resource person in the field of cultural geography to work with faculty. For cultural geographers, place offers "a way of understanding the world" (Cresswell 2007, 11). As their scholarly work attends to the significance of habits, repetitive practices and "seemingly mundane activities" (82) that invest space with meaning, cultural geographers can help theological faculties understand in new ways the creative responsibility of their institutions.

The shift from machine to organism as a metaphor for institutions changes not only the way one views leadership but also the setting of the institution itself. The machine metaphor tends to view the setting of the institution as a static location, established by a set of "fixed, objective co-ordinates" (7). Viewed as an organism, however, the setting of the seminary takes on the far richer connotations of a habitat, complete with fluctuations of energy, competing life forms, and shifting resources. In the machine metaphor, the activity of the institution is seen as self-enclosed, while the habitat metaphor suggests a broader, more complex range of interactions with forces beyond as well as within the seminary walls. Beyond the objective sense of "location," the resources of cultural geography give added attention to "locale"—the material culture of the surrounding area and its distinctive features, as well as to the "sense of place" that explores the "emotional attachments" (7) and the intersubjective feel of the institution and its wider orbit of relations.

The first portion of the day's work should surface problems with the machine metaphor and introduce the faculty to the institution-as-organism metaphor. Drawing on the resources of cultural geography, a presenter might call attention to the difference between the terms "landscape" and a "lived sense of place" to help faculty members see their institutional setting differently. Landscape, a key term to cultural geographers, refers to a place viewed from a distance as well as from a particular perspective—as in landscape painting. Hence, landscape refers to the kind of ideological judgments or assumptions about a place that may or may not be true at all when contrasted with a more empirically close "lived sense of place." Thus, a presenter might ask seminary faculty members, educated in university divinity schools, questions like the following:

- When you interviewed for a teaching post at this seminary, how did you view seminaries as institutional settings?
- Did you want to teach in a seminary?
- Did you think of it as a step down professionally or as a starting point from which to move higher?
- What about the wider cultural habitat of the seminary (such as the Bible Belt or the West Coast)?
- How did those wider settings influence your landscape perception of the institution?

One might follow up such landscape questions with others asking about the lived feel of the habitat—both of the school and the wider community. For example, faculty might be asked, "How did the lived experience of visiting the seminary and then teaching here confirm or challenge your landscape assumptions?"

Questions about landscape and the lived sense of a place will inevitably raise questions about the boundaries—physical, psychological, social, and ideological—that frame the emergent life and reach of the seminary.

- Who feels at home within the space of the seminary's approach to theological education?
- Who feels out of place or homeless within it?
- How rigid are the social boundaries of the institution—as established by denominational allegiance, social class, income level, race, and the ideological assumptions (such as conservative, liberal, or radical) of the student body or the faculty?
- By what strategies does the institution reinforce certain boundaries or seek to make others permeable?
- What types of boundaries did the school once assume to be permanent but which later became quite permeable or simply

eviscerated? How has the school responded over the years to new forms of mobility in media and culture?

- For example, in what ways has that surrounding habitat moved far more quickly than the institution, thus threatening the life of the institution for not adapting its behavior and practices?
- Conversely, in what ways has the surrounding cultural habitat been slow to move, thus threatening the institution if it moves too quickly?

After a morning of immersing the faculty in the workings of the organism/habitat metaphor and its institutional entailments, the afternoon should have two sessions, each of about ninety minutes, that begin to turn the focus of the day toward the kinds of adaptive changes facing the seminary. During the first afternoon session, the president, along with the director of development, should lay out for the faculty the set of issues challenging the well-being or even survival of the seminary in its current institutional habitat. Relating these institutional challenges to the work of teaching and learning, the dean, or consultant for the day, should help the faculty connect those larger habitat pressures to emerging anxieties felt within the classroom and shouldered by the faculty: theological and racial diversity, additional degree programs, and course offerings with virtual 24/7 availability.

In a second session that moves toward closure for the day, a faculty member, well versed in the life of the school and who has been involved in planning the event, should take a portion of the school's history—the last fifteen to twenty years, for example—and examine that history through the lens of an organism adapting to its environment, calling to mind the kinds of pressures on the school's leadership and faculty over that period of time. The presenter should then locate various conflicts both within the school itself and between the institution and various constituencies—for example, decisions with respect to curriculum, additional degree programs, increasing student diversity, and so on, within that field of pressures. By locating those decisions and faculty actions within the terrain of such felt pressures, the presenter shifts the meaning of those past actions from mere institutional history to implied adaptive strategies. Seeing the institutional life of the school through the lens of the organism/habitat metaphor can help the faculty begin to practice a way of looking at the set of problems confronting them in a more dynamic way. They are not simply the victim of cultural forces; they have the ability to help shape those forces.

Day Two—Facing Challenges of Adaptive Change: An Analogical Imagination

As deans and presidents begin to surface the range of institutional pressures requiring adaptive changes, it is crucial that they help faculty members see and experience these challenges with both realism and hope. That theological schools are not alone in facing pressures that undermine their institutional habitats can offer far more than a sense of cold comfort. The efforts of an orchestra or museum to survive in a rapidly changing environment can inspire as well as inform the faculty's own creativity and courage as a cooperative team and jump-start faculty participation in the process of institutional learning.

Local cultural and service organizations are all being pressed to become more public and justify their existence to new audiences. In the early stages of preparing for this intensive three-day period of institutional learning, the dean should be in touch with the leaders of several such organizations with an eye toward inviting one of them to participate in the seminary's process of institutional learning. The organization should be different enough so as to tap into the curiosity of the theological faculty, yet similar enough—at least in its problems—to enable the faculty to imagine a range of analogous responses to the pressures facing the school.

Following a round of exploratory conversations, the dean should ask the leader of the institution that is responding most creatively to its own habitat challenges if she or he—along with a professional member of the organization—would be willing to host the faculty for a day and illustrate the effect of the institution's creative responses to its own adaptive challenges. By situating Day Two within the space of an analogous institution, the dean reinforces what faculty members learned about the nature of habitats in Day One but also suggests that institutional learning requires fieldwork beyond the seminary library or classroom.

Key to the faculty's learning on Day Two should be the opportunity to attend carefully to the professional craft that lies at the heart of the other institution, such as the work of a cellist in a symphony orchestra or that of a curator making selections for, or even installing, a new art exhibit. Enabling faculty members to connect with the artistry of another profession should remind faculty members of the artistic craft at the heart of their own work, thus preparing them to listen with a better analogical ear to the day's conversations.

The first session of the day (ninety minutes to two hours) should include a welcome from the director of the host institution, a quick tour of the facilities, and most importantly, the chance for the faculty to enjoy observing one or more of the organization's professionals working for at least thirty to forty minutes. Following a short break, the institution's director and lead fund raising/outreach person should facilitate a second session (about ninety minutes) in which they describe for the gathered faculty the kinds of systemic and structural pressures facing their profession as a whole and their organization in particular. Vital to that discussion should be the director's willingness to share a sense of the institution's difficulties as well as its experimental attempts to increase its public visibility and strengthen its public voice. It would be especially helpful for faculty to hear about the experiments that failed and how the institution processed the lessons learned from those failures.

The director should spend about half of the session discussing how the organization has changed or refocused its working assumptions about its mission and purpose and how those changed assumptions have generated new commitments with respect to altered staffing needs, changes in programming, additional public-relations efforts, and so on.

As with Day One, Day Two should have two afternoon sessions. The morning session should have provided more than enough stimulation for lunchtime conversation, and the plan for the day should include enough time for faculty members to enjoy not only their meal but also a brisk walk in a garden or around the block.

During the first afternoon session (about one hour), the seminary faculty should hear from at least one professional member of the staff (ideally, the same person or persons observed at the outset of the day), who will describe how the systemic pressures facing the organization affected its professional members, particularly their sense of vocation. Allowing thirty to forty minutes for the professional's presentation, the remaining time should be reserved for the faculty to ask questions, particularly regarding the professional's current sense of engagement with new and traditional publics.

In the second session of the afternoon, the dean or discussion leader might ask the director to stay in the room and participate in the faculty's conversation in response to what they, as theological faculty, have seen and heard throughout the day. Because the presentations by themselves should have been deeply thought-provoking, this second session may not need to be longer than thirty or forty-five minutes. The dean or discussion leader might begin the session with questions like the following:

1. While the strength of an analogy can be difficult to assess, what have you heard today that either disturbs or stirs your own confidence in our seminary's future?
2. Given the kinds of adaptive changes we have seen and heard discussed today, what kinds of adaptive changes might we as a faculty need to address over the next few years?

Day Three—Reimagining Our Internal and Public Commitments

The analogical encounter of Day Two is particularly important for faculty members to grasp the urgency of the challenges facing the seminary and the creative possibilities for personal and institutional renewal that those challenges represent. Day Three involves the faculty in three vitally important but difficult processes of adaptive learning:

1. Naming the constituencies in the school's habitat/context
2. Being realistic about obligations to those constituencies
3. Thinking theologically about
   - an ethos of faith and reason
   - stewardship as a commitment to enhance the school's public presence and voice
   - vocation as a personal and a corporate calling

Here I propose approaching both of these processes indirectly—at least initially—by further surfacing, and challenging, a key aspect of the machine metaphor that affects the institution's assumptions about learning in an M.Div. program, namely the tendency to view it as a temporal structure.

Seminaries typically understand their curricula in temporal terms—a three-year program, first-year students vs. third-year students, midterms, finals, and all the various phrasings about which week of the semester assignments are due, all of which are understood around the axis of time. Even this faculty-development proposal's three-day structure draws on the temporal model. The danger with these temporal perceptions is that when governed by a machine metaphor of the organization, the academic program appears as an automatic process. Students and faculty both assume that interdisciplinary integration, spiritual formation, and leadership development will all happen naturally during the course of the program. They don't.

In the first session of the day, the dean or discussion leader should surface the problem with viewing the M.Div. primarily through the lens of time and suggest that the faculty explore the possibilities of viewing the M.Div. curriculum in spatial terms, as a place of engagement with and commitment to various constituencies. In making such a proposal, the dean should link the spatial imagery of "habitats" to another spatial image, that of "context"—a term shaping virtually every discipline related to theological study. Pressing the matter further, the dean could point out that current ATS standards ask schools to reflect upon the context of student learning. By context, the ATS refers not only to questions of globalization and discourses "from the margins" but also to the cultural setting of the institution itself within which most of its graduates will take up some form of ministry. By asking about the kind of contextual spaces that the M.Div. curriculum both inhabits and creates, the dean or discussion leader can then ask the faculty about the variety of constituencies and institutions, as well as the variety of students, with whom the space of the curriculum is shared.

Dividing the faculty into small groups, ask the following kinds of questions:

- How does the seminary understand itself and commit itself—as an institution—to these differing contexts and constituencies?
- How does that institutional understanding and commitment express itself in the M.Div. curriculum?

The discussion leader should ask the small groups to name those institutions, religious and cultural, that provide the seminary not only with sustainable financial resources and a sustainable applicant pool but also with a range of ministerial settings within which its graduates will practice some form of ministry. Framing the question in this way illuminates not only what the seminary receives from its habitat but also what it contributes to that habitat—namely, graduates and resources for theological reflection upon church and society.

While the reporting from the various groups should surface a variety of civic organizations, such as hospitals and foundations, universities and colleges, and social services agencies, they should also return, time and again, to its affiliated denominational body and to congregations—those belonging to the denomination and to other denominations as well. The discussion leader should then follow up by asking the groups to clarify the contexts of those congregations: Are they rural, urban, or suburban? Are they megachurches, large churches, or small churches?

The questions—and the answers—may seem simplistic at first, but they reveal significant illusions and fault lines within the faculty, collectively and individually. As we saw with Day Two's visit to an artistic institution, habitat pressures raise basic questions about institutional identity and commitment. Habitat pressures also surface uncomfortable evidence that the audiences which the organization has simply assumed would always be supportive are themselves no longer so, or are themselves struggling and cannot afford to be as supportive as they once were. How many congregations, or civic organizations for that matter, the discussion leader might ask, would recognize the seminary as an important conversation partner in ministry or service to the community?

In his discussion of "surfacing and testing mental models," Senge notes the important distinction between "espoused theory from theory in use" (14). His point is helpful here. While all faculty members will affirm the "mission statement" of the seminary in broad terms and express real commitment to both ministry and the life of congregations, many faculty members spend relatively little time either exploring the institutional lives of various congregations connected to the school—through students, alumni, or donors—or engaging the content of their disciplines with the contextual settings actually faced by seminary students. I raise the point because foregrounding congregations as sharing in the space of the curriculum—and not just as a background institution in the school's habitat—will surface anxiety and resistance in a percentage of faculty members, even fine faculty members.

The question about congregational connections is an uncomfortable one, because for a significant number of faculty members teaching in denominational seminaries, the experience of doctoral study with its attending critical methodologies alienated them from what Paul Ricoeur would call faith's first naiveté and, therefore, from the churches in which they were born and raised. Suspicious of the church's tendencies toward provincialism, racial bigotry, and anti-intellectualism, all wrapped in illusions of moral superiority, many seminary faculty members remain at the margins of congregational life. Not deeply in touch with the contextual and congregational nuances of where their students are engaged in ministry, seminary professors can prepare students for churches that do not exist.

Deans and discussion leaders, therefore, must be prepared for significant resistance from faculty members who may think that closer linkage to congregations will dumb down the curriculum, leading the seminary in the direction of a trade school. Similar to the anxiety among professional orchestra musicians and conductors that an orchestra is lowering its standards in order to appeal to a larger public audience, this particular anxiety is rooted in the assumption that the faculty member's primary allegiance is, and should be, to her or his professional discipline.

Such cautionary advice has its place, but so does Senge's principle of "creative tension." Even if all faculty and administration members agree on the kind of habitat they would like to have, they still must face and engage the reality of their habitat as it is, thus juxtaposing their vision with their current reality. In addition, faculty critiques of congregational life are sometimes prone to overstate the dire conditions of congregational decline. Deans and discussion leaders can point to recent work by Diana Butler Bass (2004; 2006; and Bass and Steward-Sicking 2005), among others, that describes significant evidence of life and vitality among denominational congregations. They can point as well to various denominational commitments to invest significantly in new church starts. While the seminary curriculum can also open onto a closer engagement with the civic institutions of public life, significant institutional energy must inevitably go toward reconnecting and deepening the seminary ties to congregational and denominational audiences. Such a conclusion is not simply strategic but theological as well.

The second portion of the day's work should help faculty members think theologically about the adaptive challenges facing the school and themselves as teachers and learners. Insofar as the three-day project is drawing to a close with this session, the dean should lead these final discussions.

Returning to Senge's emphasis on the role of creative tension in learning organizations (9), the dean should frame the following final conversations as a series of creative theological tensions.

With denominational seminaries in particular, it is important that faculties not be split between those committed to a purely academic vision of their disciplines and those committed to ministry. For many denominational seminaries, speaking of a creative tension of "faith-and-reason" might prove helpful as a way of avoiding the more polarizing positions of "faithful reason" (as represented by the large evangelical schools) and "reasoned faith" (as embodied by university divinity schools). Rather than privileging one term over the other, denominational seminaries are called to hold these two curricular desires in tension, responding to the present needs of churches while also developing attitudes and skills needed for the future viability and integrity of Christian communities.

Along with the creative tension of faith and reason in preparing women and men for ministry in the church and in society, a second theological framework to be discussed is that of stewardship. By this point in the three-day process, all faculty members should recognize that the adaptive challenges facing them will require new kinds of institutional learning on their part—including implications for the evaluation of the current faculty as well as for identifying important qualifications in new faculty members. In a time of institutional rebuilding—in the work of reconnecting with congregations and opening up new conversations with secular and social services organizations—faculty commitment to engaging in the kinds of learning that strengthen the institution will become a more significant factor in the areas of tenure review and promotion than it had been in the past. Such learning will involve much more than additional classroom or online teaching; it will require participation in various kinds of fieldwork, of becoming personally familiar with various communities and contexts that share the space of the seminary's curriculum. As I once heard Dan Aleshire say at a theology and vocation workshop: "The saying used to be publish or perish; now it is get public or perish."

Conclusion

Finally, the dean on Day Three needs to help faculty members reflect on the creative tension between their personal vocations and that of the seminary's vocation as a theological institution. For many doctoral students at university divinity schools, acquiring a full-time position—at any institution—can seem like confirmation of one's vocation as a teacher and scholar. Too frequently, however, professional reflection upon one's own vocation and its fit within an institution's vocation does not proceed much further.

One tends to assume, or hope, that one's interests as a teacher and scholar align with the interests and mission of one's theological school. Worse, one avoids or denies the conflict between one's interests and those of the institution. Frequently confused themselves about their institution's actual identity, administrators and rank-and-tenure committees often fail to say clearly what they expect of new faculty members with respect to institutional commitment.

One positive benefit of the institutional-habitat crisis facing many seminaries is that it should urge deans and rank-and-tenure committees to find better ways of introducing new faculty members to the institutional and vocational ethos of their schools. Such exercises might also help tenured faculty members to discern in new ways their own vocational calling. If we are converted not once but many times in our lives, as I have been told Thomas Merton once suggested, then we have reason to hope that the Holy Spirit might be at work in the difficult processes of adaptive change that move us both institutionally and personally to clarify our vocational and professional commitments.

Notes

1. The amount of endowment generating funds for operations currently stands at $6.7 million.
2. Chaves (1999, 180) asserts that the "flush" 1950s was something of an anomaly in the financial history of American religion, and he points out that "black church leaders do not seem to experience the present financial state of African American churches as qualitatively different from the past. I think this is because black church leaders did not experience a period of unusual plenty against which the present looks bad. There is no bust unless one first has a boom."
3. Chaves (1999), in the title essay of *Financing American Religion*, suggests that what appears as a financial crisis in denominational seminaries may reflect a participation crisis (171–172).
4. For an essay detailing the history of the consortium movement, which began in 1943 with the Federated Theological Faculty of the University of Chicago, see Berling (1992).
5. See Sevier's interview of Jack Trout (Trout 2006). At one point in the interview, Sevier asks, "What is the most important thing that colleges and universities need to understand about brand marketing?" Trout answers: "They need to answer the question, *What is our difference?* What is the reason that people should attend our institution rather than the 'other' institution. That is what a brand truly is" (3). Earlier in the interview, Trout argues against doing more things in favor of specializing: "If you focus on something of value, and become truly good at it, the marketplace will reward you. . . . Specialization is the only effective weapon against bigger players who probably can do almost everything" (2).
6. Carroll, Wheeler, Aleshire, and Marler (1997) studied two seminaries, which they refer to pseudonymously as "Evangelical" and "Mainline," respectively. They

demonstrated that not only evangelical but also more liberal and progressive schools develop identity profiles.

7. Some denominations have imposed requirements for students to spend at least one year of study during their M.Div. degree program at one of the denominational seminaries.

8. Bible colleges have also played a significant role over time in evangelical circles, providing a significant pool of applicants for evangelical seminaries. Today, however, one also sees a variety of alternative approaches to theological education. Bible institutes, for example, which do not offer either undergraduate or graduate level courses, offer certificate programs in biblical studies to Latino students, in their own language, that qualify them for ordination in many Latino churches. In addition, a number of Korean-American denominations (headquartered in Korea but with "presbyteries" or "districts" in the U.S.) as well as some large Korean-American churches in the U. S. have sponsored their own graduate-level seminaries that typically hold evening classes led by established and seasoned clergy.

9. To be sure, some denominational seminaries—those with campus housing and heavily funded scholarship programs—have also been able to maintain a relatively young student pool.

10. To learn more about William J. Baumol and his analysis, see Baumol and Towse (1997).

11. See Chaves's concluding reflections in the title essay of *Financing American Religion* in which he raises the analogy of religious organizations to nonprofit ones. "In the present context, an important decision faced by many religious organizations is whether or not to turn to the larger nonprofit world and its ways of understanding, seeking, and managing material resources" (1999, 181).

12. Fifty of the 251 ATS schools (or 20 percent) report nothing for long-term investments, thus complicating any attempt at an accurate assessment of the wealth gap in ATS schools. ATS staff members Nancy Merrill and Chris Meinzer provide several cautions when interpreting long-term investment figures: (1) the figures are self-reported by the schools; (2) portions of long-term investments may be restricted, and, therefore, the total of such investments may not fully indicate institutional health; and (3) many evangelical Protestant seminaries do not believe in having endowments or have only recently shifted to holding such long-term investments.

13. Investment firm president Herbert A. Allen, in a December 21, 2007, *New York Times* op-ed piece, "Gold in the Ivory Tower," describes the wider educational crisis: "In the realm of education,...there's a particularly corrosive shift that's taking place, one that has tremendous consequences for the development of America's best minds: the growing gap between super-wealthy colleges and universities—and the rest of the academic world. There is a widening division that gives top colleges and universities a huge financial advantage over their poorer counterparts." His creative proposal is to "tax the investment income of the wealthiest colleges (though not their endowments). If the endowments of all academic institutions were evaluated on a per student basis, a standard could be set that could begin to allow revenue sharing....An example: Harvard or Williams (my alma mater) have endowments that are well over $500,000 per student. Why not take the colleges whose endowments exceed that per student amount and tax their capital gains? The tax revenue could then be put into a designated pool and distributed pro rata to colleges under the base level. The college with the lowest per student endowment would get the highest share." See also Karen

W. Arenson's February 4, 2008 *New York Times* article, "Endowments Widen a Higher Education Gap," in which she reports "how the wealth amassed by elite universities like Princeton through soaring endowments over the past decade has exacerbated the divide between a small group of spectacularly wealthy universities and all others. If Harvard has $34.9 billion or Yale $22.5 billion, fewer than 400 of the roughly 4,500 colleges and universities in the United States had even $100 million in endowments in the fiscal year that ended in June. Most had less than $10 million."

14. For a study assessing the dangers of student debt in theological education, see Ruger and Wheeler (1995).

15. See McLean (1996a, 1996b, 1999) for reflections on the pressures, challenges, and promise of both the deanship and presidency in Protestant denominational seminaries. In McLean, for example, one sees the dean's office dealing with the results of Baumol's cost disease: "Deans most often cited 'time and money' or, rather the lack of both as hindrances to them in doing their job.... Second only to insufficient time were concerns about limited financial resources and the constraints placed on their efforts to strengthen programs and develop the faculty. Third, and closely related to the first two, was the lack of adequate support staff to assist the dean and to ease the workload of the office.... Fourth, deans felt hindered by a variety of institutional problems distinctive to their particular settings, ranging from weaknesses within the administration to aspects of the culture, such as lack of collegiality, distrust, and turf wars, that had become barriers to their work. Some deans felt hampered by their personal inability to manage the workload and deal with these other institutional issues" (1999, 240).

16. Given the figures I cited earlier about the distribution of wealth (long-term investments) among ATS schools, Farley might have been even more pessimistic about the possibilities of genuine change. The relative wealth of the large university divinity schools inoculates them against the effects of Baumol's cost disease and thus against the kind of pressures to which smaller, less prestigious schools have been responding for decades.

17. See Warford (2004, ix-xii) for a discussion of The Lexington Seminar process.

18. Deans may feel the need to spread these sessions out over two semesters, but each day of the model is intended to build on one another, and the required momentum can all too easily be sidetracked if the sessions are spread over an extended period.

19. While I present each of the major steps of the model as occurring in a single day, deans might find it profitable to structure the activities (particularly those of the retreat) over two days or perhaps a day and a half, thus providing additional time for rest and relaxation together, such as a reception and dinner the evening before. For testimony to the effectiveness of group downtime together, see the final reports from schools participating in The Lexington Seminar—lexingtonseminar.org/archives.

References

Allen, Herbert A. 2007. "Gold in the Ivory Tower." *New York Times.* December 21. http://www.nytimes.com/2007/12/21/opinion/21allen.html (accessed December 28, 2007).

Arenson, Karen W. 2008. "Endowments Widen a Higher Education Gap." *New York Times.* February 4, 2008, Education. http://www.nytimes.com/2008/02/04/education/04endowment.html (accessed February 5, 2008).

Association of Theological Schools. 2006. "Table 1.2: Significant Institutional Characteristics of Each Member School, 2005–2006." In *2005–2006 Annual Data Tables*. PDF file downloaded from http://www.ats.edu/resources/fact_book asp.

Austin Presbyterian Theological Seminary. 1999. Project Report. http://www.lexingtonseminar.org/archive/archive_doc.php/doctype/report/id/259/

Bass, Diana Butler. 2004. *The Practicing Congregation: Imagining a New Old Church*. Herndon, VA: Alban Institute.

———. 2006. *Christianity for the Rest of Us: How the Neighborhood Church is Transforming the Faith*. New York: HarperOne.

———, and Joseph Steward-Sicking, eds. 2005. *From Nomads to Pilgrims: Stories from Practicing Congregations*. Herndon, VA: Alban Institute.

Baumol, William J., and Ruth Towse, ed. 1997. *Baumol's Cost Disease: The Arts and Other Victims*. Northampton, MA: Edward Elgar Publishing.

Bennett, John. 2003. *Academic Life: Hospitality, Ethics, and Spirituality*. Bolton, MA: Anker Publishing.

Berling, Judith A. 1992. "Theological Consortia: The Creative Space between Church and University." In *Religious Studies, Theological Studies, and the University-Divinity School*, ed. Joseph Mitsuo Kitagawa, 171–196. Atlanta: Scholars Press.

Calvin Theological Seminary. 1999. Project Report. http://www.lexingtonseminar.org/archive/archive_doc.php/doctype/report/id/260/

Carroll, Jackson W., Barbara G. Wheeler, Daniel O. Aleshire, and Penny Long Marler. 1997. "A Tale of Two Seminaries." *The Christian Century* 114 (5): 126–129, 152–163.

Chaves, Mark. 1999. "Financing American Religion." In *Financing American Religion*, ed. Mark Chaves and Sharon L. Miller, 169–188. Walnut Creek, CA: AltaMira Press.

———. 2006. "Supersized: Analyzing the Trend toward Larger Churches." *The Christian Century* 123 (24): 23–24.

Claremont School of Theology. 2000. Project Report. http://www.lexingtonseminar.org/archive/archive_doc.php/doctype/report/id/266/

Cresswell, Tim. 2007. *Place: A Short Introduction*. Malden, MA: Blackwell.

Eastern Baptist Theological Seminary. 2000. Project Report. http://www.lexingtonseminar.org/archive/archive_doc.php/doctype/report/id/268/

Farley, Edward. 1997. "Why Seminaries Don't Change: A Reflection on Faculty Specialization." *The Christian Century* 114 (5): 133–143.

Handbook of Accreditation. 2006. Pittsburgh, PA: The Association of Theological Schools.

Heifetz, Ronald A. 1994. *Leadership without Easy Answers*. Cambridge, MA: Belknap Press of Harvard University Press.

Lutheran School of Theology at Chicago. 1999. Project Report. http://www.lexingtonseminar.org/archive/archive_doc.php/doctype/report/id/261/

Luther Seminary. 2001. Project Report. http://www.lexingtonseminar.org/archive/archive_doc.php/doctype/report/id/273/

Lynn, Elizabeth, and Barbara G. Wheeler. 1999. *Missing Connections: Public Perceptions of Theological Education and Religious Leadership*. Auburn Studies, no. 6. New York: Auburn Theological Seminary.

McCarthy, Kevin, Elizabeth H. Ondaatje, Laura Zakaras, Arthur Brooks. 2005. *Gifts of the Muse: Reframing the Debate about the Benefits of the Arts*. Santa Monica, CA: Rand Corporation.

McCormick Theological Seminary. 2000. Project Report. http://www.lexingtonseminar. org/archive/archive_doc.php/doctype/report/id/267/

McLean, Jeanne P. 1996a. "Leadership: The Study of the Seminary Presidency; Reflections of Seminary Leaders." *Theological Education* 32, supplement III.

———. 1996b. "The Study of Chief Academic Officers in Theological Schools: Reflections on Academic Leadership." *Theological Education* 33 (supplement), autumn.

———. 1999. *Leading from the Center: The Emerging Role of the Chief Academic Officer in Theological Schools.* Atlanta: Scholars Press.

Mendenhall, Charles and Douglas M. Ronsheim. 2006. "Expanding the Context of Care: Formation from the Inside Out and the Outside In." In *The Formation of Pastoral Counselors,* ed. Duane R. Bidwell and Joretta L. Marshall, 209–220. New York: Haworth Press.

Peluso-Verdend, Gary, and Jack Seymour. 2005. "Hearing the Congregation's Voice in Evaluating/Revising the M.Div. Curriculum: The Church Relations Council." *Theological Education* 40 (supplement): 51–62.

Ruger, Anthony. 1999. "Financing Protestant Theological Schools." In *Financing American Religion,* ed. Mark Chaves and Sharon L. Miller, 111–118. Walnut Creek, CA: AltaMira Press.

———, and Barbara G. Wheeler. 1995. *Manna from Heaven? Theological and Rabbinical Student Debt.* Auburn Studies, no. 3. New York: Auburn Theological Seminary.

Senge, Peter. 1990. "The Leader's New Work: Building Learning Organizations." Reprint Series, *Sloan Management Review* 32 (1): 7–23.

Tommasini, Anthony. 2006. "Looking for Citizens for a Few Good Orchestras." *New York Times,* December 3, AR29.

Trout, Jack. 2006. "Trout on Strategy: Differentiation in Higher Education." Stamats White Paper. Interview by Robert A. Sevier. www.stamats.com.

Virginia Theological Seminary. 1999. Project Report. http://www.lexingtonseminar. org/archive/archive_doc.php/doctype/report/id/263/

Warford, Malcolm L., ed. 2004. *Practical Wisdom: On Theological Teaching and Learning.* New York: Peter Lang Publishing.

Winnicott, Donald. 1971, 1979. *Play and Reality.* New York: Basic Books.

2. *Student Learning and Formation: An Improvisational Model*

PETER T. CHA

One of the emerging forces reshaping the nature of and approach to today's theological education is the profound change taking place in student profiles. What is clear is that today's seminary students are dramatically different from those of previous generations and that traditional practices of teaching and learning are increasingly becoming ineffective. Who, then, are these students? What are their educational needs, and how do they learn? How are today's seminaries seeking to facilitate student learning and formation? This chapter explores these and other related questions by examining the experiences and reflections of those Protestant seminaries that participated in The Lexington Seminar, 1999–2004. It then offers a model to help seminary deans and faculties engage the issue of student learning and formation.

Who Are Today's Students?

Students today are a far more heterogeneous group than they were fifty years ago. They are diverse demographically, but they are also diverse in their preparation for seminary, both intellectually and spiritually.

Diversity in Demographics, Preparation, and Expectations

Many recent studies indicate that diversity is perhaps the single most defining characteristic of today's seminary student body. According to the Association of Theological Schools of the United States and Canada (2003), the number of seminarians not of European heritage has increased from 4 percent of the total in 1977 to 22 percent in 2002. The number of women students has also sharply increased during the past three decades; in 2002, up to 36 percent of seminarians were women, an increase of 234 percent during this period. According to ATS, theological students are also more evenly distributed across the adult age span, thus making them, on average, older than students preparing for other professions, such as medicine and law. Of all M.Div. students in 2002, 45 percent were thirty-five years or older, and nearly half the students at seminaries were married. Finally, in terms of the diversity of religious traditions, interdenominational schools such as Fuller Theological Seminary attract students from more than one hundred denominations while even a denominational school such as Candler School of Theology reports thirty-six denominations represented in its student body.

These varying personal backgrounds, then, contribute to diversity in terms of what the students bring to their classrooms—different learning styles, uneven academic abilities, and varying assumptions about what they should attain from their seminary education. A recent ethnographic study of M.Div. students from seven seminaries (Siew and Peluso-Verdend 2005), for instance, indicates that the educational background of these students, such as their major in college, significantly affects their seminary learning experiences. The study also confirms that older, second-career students experience learning very differently than their younger counterparts. These variances pose many questions and challenges for theological educators who want to ensure that all students are engaged in learning and that certain groups are neither favored nor overlooked.

Finally, there is also a range of diversity in the types and contexts of ministries for which students are being prepared to serve. Recent trends indicate that a growing number of seminary graduates are looking for ministry opportunities outside of the congregational context, many choosing to serve in nonprofit or parachurch organizations while others pursue academic vocations. Furthermore, given the variety of congregations that exist in today's multicultural world, even those who seek pastoral ministry see themselves being prepared for ministry settings that are often quite different from those of their peers. Given these and other diversity factors found among today's students, it is evident that seminaries must exercise a good deal of creativity and intentionality if they are to provide optimal learning experiences for all their students.

Clearly, the increasing diversity of students has significantly challenged the task of teaching and learning in today's seminaries. It is not accidental that more than half of the teaching-learning narratives submitted by the schools that participated in The Lexington Seminar wrestled with some aspect of student diversity. However, at the same time, as a growing body of literature in multicultural education reminds us (Foster 2002), student diversity can also offer rich opportunities for schools to create and experience transformative learning. Indeed, a number of Lexington Seminar seminaries identified new opportunities for learning generated by diversity and demonstrated their intention to use such opportunities to transform not just the lives of their students but also their institution's self-understanding of its identity and mission.

Diversity in Formation

Another significant characteristic of today's seminarians is that many are not familiar with their own church and theological traditions. Not having had significant formation experiences in church, home, or community, many of these students struggle to understand their theological and vocational identities, increasingly expecting their seminaries to provide them with basic formational experiences which, in the past, had been offered by local congregations. In addition, as Raymond Williams (2004, 21) observed, due partly to life experiences often characterized by "brokenness," many of today's students struggle to maintain and reinforce their personal identities. These student characteristics make it necessary for seminaries not only to reassess their current practices in the area of student formation but also of teaching and learning in general and integrative learning in particular.

In the past, when students came to seminary having been "formed" in their Christian homes and local congregations, being immersed in seminary life may have sufficiently reinforced their spiritual formation journey; in such a context, seminaries may not have felt the need to develop specific programs explicitly for their students' formation. A faculty member in the narrative of the Church Divinity School of the Pacific (2001) recalled, "In fact, the traditional Anglican seminary approach has been described as 'formation by osmosis,' because so much of it has to do with studying and praying together in community." Given the needs of today's students, however, many seminaries are recognizing that formation by osmosis and other passive approaches no longer serve their students well. Seminaries need to find ways to invite their students to participate in well-designed formation experiences that prepare them for their future ministries.

The increasing diversity among students also challenges seminaries to examine their traditional assumptions about student formation. In the past, when denominational seminaries drew the majority of faculty and students from the same denominational background, formation by osmosis might have been possible. However, in today's setting of diversity, especially as denominational schools are increasingly attracting faculty members and students from other theological traditions, such an approach to formation is no longer feasible. Seminaries, then, faced with the reality of increasing diversity and of serving students with greater formation needs, are searching for ways to incorporate formation into their formal curriculum and the wider institutional life.

In *Educating Clergy* (2006), Charles Foster and colleagues argue that formation is at the center of educating clergy because compared with the education in other professions, the training of clergy is particularly concerned about "meaning, purpose and identity" (8). Educating clergy, they assert, should be far more than the acquisition of knowledge or even cognitive tools, for its primary aim is to enable the student to become a person who thinks, feels, and acts a certain way. How do seminaries, then, aim to foster among their diverse students what Dykstra (2001, 2–3) calls "pastoral imagination"? How do student diversity and the activity of student learning-formation intersect in today's seminary settings?

I intend to address these questions by examining the activities of specific Lexington Seminar schools in the areas of listening, integrative learning, and student formation. In today's diverse classrooms, settings in which faculty members cannot assume that all students have similar needs and wants as learners, an intentional and methodical practice of listening to students becomes an increasingly significant pedagogical activity, a kind of listening that can further inform and even reshape faculty members' understanding of teaching and learning. The increasing diversity among students also prompts seminaries to be attentive to the importance of integrative learning, a type of learning that enables adult students to grow in their ability to integrate their knowledge, skills, moral integrity, and religious commitments so that they learn how to, among other things, contextualize their learning to experiences of their own particular faith communities. Similarly, responding to the reality that their students come with widely varying ecclesiastical and life experiences, many seminaries are also placing a growing emphasis on their students' formation, encouraging their students to be attentive to the process of their development as a whole person, the process of bringing together "one's intellectual, emotional, and spiritual development into a wise, coherent whole" (Winkelmes 2005, 162). These three activities of listening, integrative learning, and student formation, then, represent today's seminaries' response to the challenge of growing diversity among their students. These activities are, in many ways, interconnected and intertwined. In this chapter, however, I examine each separately, studying how each of these activities is cultivated and practiced in individual seminary settings.

Knowing Our Students

Assuming that the first rule of good teaching is to know our students, the administrators and faculty at Claremont School of Theology (CST) chose as their Lexington Seminar project to investigate how their students learn to embrace faith and reason, and how they deconstruct and then reconstruct their beliefs in light of what they are learning in their M.Div. program. Given the dizzying array of cultural and theological diversity in its student body, the team participating in The Lexington Seminar recognized the possibility that diverse students might experience this process diversely. Therefore, the team decided that their critical assessment of the M.Div. curriculum must include the practice of listening to their students more fully than they had done to date.

Developing a Culture of Listening

During the 2000–2001 academic year, two of the Lexington team members—a Latina faculty member who teaches religious education and a male faculty member of European heritage who teaches church administration—volunteered to facilitate a systematic listening project. At the beginning of the school year, these faculty members selected seven first-year M.Div. students who reflected the diversity in Claremont's student body; they decided to interview first-year students because these students seem to experience the most angst in adjusting to their new learning environment and in processing what they are learning. Throughout the year, the group met four times; each group interview session began with the question, "Tell us about your experience so far at Claremont," inviting students to express their thoughts and feelings while the faculty members sat and listened. Because their desire was to empower students to voice their concerns and expectations freely, the faculty team decided to interview these students in a group setting rather than individually since the latter might be too intimidating for some students. Because the faculty facilitators' desire was to encourage the students to identify and name key issues that demand the school's attention, they also minimized their own participation by asking questions of clarification only. Furthermore, because both faculty facilitators participated in each session and because they came from different backgrounds, they hoped to minimize the possibility of mishearing or misinterpreting what the students expressed.

After each session, both faculty members spent long hours reviewing the videotapes and the transcripts of the interviews, noting the verbal and nonverbal communication that took place during each session. They identified themes and categories that surfaced repeatedly and possible connections among them. At the start of each subsequent meeting, the facilitators asked the student group to verify what the facilitators had heard and what they had identified as key issues and themes.

Through these listening sessions, the faculty interview leaders had an opportunity to hear these students' learning experiences on their own terms, and they presented the summary of their findings (both critical of the school and complimentary) at a faculty retreat in which the wider faculty community was beginning its dialogue about the revisioning of the M.Div. curriculum.

Although the time invested in the systematic listening project made it a costly process, the two faculty participants believe the project made many significant contributions to the seminary. It helped the faculty community attain a more complete and accurate understanding of their students' educational goals and needs as well as an honest assessment of the students' own learning experiences. While the findings from this project may not have contributed to immediate changes, they nonetheless generated numerous "parking lot" conversations among the faculty that eventually entered into official faculty deliberations, thus shaping academic programs and policies.

For the seven participating students, the project was an empowering experience. For those students from historically marginalized groups, the project was particularly meaningful, encouraging them to become more invested in the institutional mission and identity of Claremont, to become more fully engaged members of their learning community. For example, one of the student participants, an African American woman, has graduated and is now serving on the school's board of trustees.

Even more significant, perhaps, the project has played a strategic role in creating a culture of listening at Claremont. After the completion of the project and as the faculty continued curriculum revisioning during the subsequent years, the school continued its practice of listening to students by hosting multiple town meetings with larger groups of students. Then in 2006, partly in an effort to make listening activities more consistent and permanent, the Claremont faculty adopted a portfolio approach to assessment, aiming to assess not only each student's learning progress but also to hear how each student is experiencing his or her education at Claremont. At the end of each year, the faculty members read all of their student advisees' portfolios and look for patterns and themes that emerge in their students' reflections, an interpretive process developed by their two colleagues who led the earlier systematic listening project. In this manner, student portfolios are intentionally utilized as listening tools as all faculty members participate in the assessment of the school's effectiveness in teaching and learning, further reinforcing the school's emerging culture of listening.

Reflections on Claremont's Approach to Listening

Given the diversity and rapid change in today's student profiles, each seminary needs to cultivate ways to listen to its students, particularly how they experience learning and formation in the school. The Claremont experience provides weighty support for the value of such practices. Furthermore, it also demonstrates how a school can utilize an ethnographic interview method as a tool to listen to its diverse students and how such a practice can even promote certain educational and cultural changes within the learning institution.

However, in order for such a listening process to be fruitful, certain conditions must exist and a certain ethos must be in place. Does the school embrace and practice values such as mutuality and dialogue? To put it more directly, do faculty members want to hear about the students' experiences? If not, the dean and the faculty community members must first foster and strengthen such values among themselves so that the practice of listening will produce constructive and meaningful results.

Furthermore, if a school establishes a project to encourage a particular change in institutional culture, the project must be accompanied and followed by other similar events and projects. When the systematic listening project was being implemented, Claremont's newly hired director of spiritual formation also conducted his own yearlong listening project, which included attending first-year M.Div. classes and listening to students in those classes, focusing particularly on their spiritual formation experiences. When the listening project team brought their report to the faculty retreat on curriculum revisioning, the director of spiritual formation also brought his, thus making a deeper impression about the significance of listening to their students. After this experience of listening, Claremont faculty members decided to sponsor and support other forms of listening, thus nurturing and reinforcing its new culture of listening.

Finally, Claremont's experience demonstrates that another key value of the practice of listening is that it energizes and sustains significant conversations about teaching and listening among different constituents in the seminary community, whether in the parking lot or in the boardroom. As students' reflections and experiences become a significant piece of these conversations, they not only help the faculty do their task better but also reshape the school's understanding of mission and identity. In this way, then, the formation of students and the formation of the seminary itself become dialectically intertwined, the formation experience of one reflexively shaping that of the other.

Integrative Learning: Learning to See How Things Fit

Given the diversity of today's students and their formation needs just discussed, a growing body of literature on theological education asserts that today's seminaries need to see student learning as a process of integrating one's intellectual, emotional, and spiritual development into a coherent whole. Victor Klimoski and colleagues suggest that such an integration-oriented education should engage students in the areas of theological knowledge, pastoral practice, and Christian identity "in ways that raise to a new level of consciousness what it means to see things whole" (Klimoski, O'Neil, and Schuth 2005, 49–51). This approach, Klimoski notes, would produce learners who can, among other things, respond to new and different challenges wisely and who can effectively serve in diverse settings of ministry.

There are indications that today's seminaries are paying more attention to integrative student learning (Foster et al. 2006, 7). Nonetheless, some of the narratives of The Lexington Seminar schools reveal that meaningful integration is not yet a reality experienced by many seminarians. In Austin Presbyterian Theological Seminary's narrative (1999), a frustrated part-time seminarian complains to the dean, "It's just hard to see how it all 'fits together' from this side of the degree." Similarly, in their listening sessions, Claremont students voice their concerns and yearning in the following way: "What does this class or this program have to do with why I am at CST? What does it have to do with my life's meaning and direction? We want to be able to bring ourselves to the material we are learning" (Claremont 2000, 9).

Among those schools that participated in The Lexington Seminar, however, a few seminaries have made a strong institutional commitment to embrace integration as the key approach to their theological education. In doing so, these schools have intentionally introduced new models of learning that have impacted not only their students but also the teaching activities of their teachers and the wider institutional structure. The following section explores the recent experiences of United Theological Seminary of the Twin Cities (UTS), identifying some key steps it took to develop a new model of learning that focuses on integration.

Embracing Integrative Learning: An Institutional Experience

Recognizing that the process of developing an effective integrative education cannot be relegated to a department or a group of faculty members, the faculty and administrators of UTS saw early on that their goal of developing an integration-oriented theological education would require an institutional commitment and willingness to change. They, therefore, articulated one of their main goals as "institutional transformation to better foster integration in its various dimensions for all United Seminary students in ways that take account of diverse locations" (UTS 2001b, 1).

In 2001, the faculty gathered at a retreat to discuss and establish a shared understanding of what integration means to the UTS community.

A faculty member who designed and led the faculty discussions began the process by asking the question, "What would an excellent graduate with a M.Div. look like?" When different small groups of faculty produced their own list of qualities, the faculty leader took these lists and categorized them, then presented them back to the faculty for further conversation. What emerged from this process was the Indicators of Integration, a list of ten indicators[1] to provide the framework through which the faculty can evaluate their students' abilities to integrate. Examples of the indicators include the following:

- The student demonstrates accountability for their own learning process and decisions.
- The student is able to understand and articulate both the particularity of their own (cultural, familial, religious, personal) story as well as its resonances and dissonances with others' stories, and with larger, social, religious, and cultural narratives.
- The student is able to articulate their own theology of ministry, drawing on the core curricular areas.
- When faced with an unexpected situation in ministry, the student is able to respond effectively. The response will reflect the consideration of context, culture, theology of ministry, and the appropriate arts of ministry. (2003)

Once adopted by the faculty council in 2002, the Indicators of Integration began to influence not only how each individual faculty member approached teaching but also began to reshape how the faculty viewed and discussed the school's curricular design. Previously, M.Div. students had been required to take the integrative exam during their final year in the program, a paper assignment that asks students to analyze a dilemma or situation from their own ministry experience. Each paper is read by two faculty members and the student's field supervisor, seeking to assess the student's ability to integrate classroom and ministry. However, as the school's narrative (UTS 2001a) indicates, some students were frustrated because they felt underprepared and because students from different backgrounds had different understandings of what "integration" meant. Using the Indicators of Integrations as their evaluative tool, the UTS faculty concluded that the integrative exam was not an adequate educational method and decided to replace it with the Integrative Notebook, which is designed to provide students with an ongoing context for reflection, evaluation, and integration (the structure of the Notebook is discussed later).

The school also redesigned how the faculty advisors evaluate their student advisees. Under the new system, faculty members extensively evaluate each advisee annually, reviewing sections of the student's Integrative Notebook and discussing with the student how she or he has been growing in different areas of integration. In order to prepare for these sessions, faculty members often invite input from their colleagues in assessing their student advisees. A good portion of faculty meetings are often devoted to the topic of integration, frequently focusing on certain students who are visibly struggling with the process. These formal and informal conversations, in turn, reinforce the significance of integration to the faculty and enable it to gain a stronger institutional footing.

The institution's commitment to integration also led the faculty to explore ways to redesign the curriculum to assist students in fostering integration across disciplines. As a result of their conversations and deliberations, the faculty decided to place a greater emphasis on team teaching, offering opportunities for faculty members from different backgrounds to model interdisciplinary conversation and integration. In addition, the school decided to add several new courses that focus on different aspects of integration; three of these courses are required for all M.Div. students.

Finally, another significant institutional change was to grant faculty status to the seminary chaplain, inviting her to be a permanent member of the faculty council. Given that integrative learning is a holistic process that goes beyond formal classroom interactions, the school recognized that the chaplain plays a greater role in the new educational paradigm, and that her voice was needed in the faculty conversation. In so doing, the institution's commitment to integrative learning also contributed to another form of integration, namely the structural integration of the institution.

Embracing Integrative Learning: Students' Experiences

One of the important aspects of adult learning is that it is a self-directed process (Brookfield 1986; Merriam and Caffarella 1999). This is particularly true for integration-oriented adult learning (Klimoski, O'Neil, and Schuth 2005, 63–65). While a school such as UTS might make a concerted effort to offer a positive setting for integrative learning, if students are not convinced of its value or do not take ownership of the process, the outcome of this educational approach will be uncertain at best. Given this potential challenge, how does UTS seek to invite students to engage in the collaborative learning process?

When new students come to UTS, the school clearly highlights integration as one of the centerpieces of its educational process, describing what the school means by integration as well as explaining how students might achieve and experience integration. New students then receive an orientation about the Integrative Notebook through their academic advisors as well as in their first of the three required integration courses. The following are some of the required components of the Integrative Notebook:

- After-course reflection sheets for each course the student has taken.
- A summary sheet synthesizing each year's student-advisor assessment of the student's progress in relation to the Indicators of Integration.
- Copies of the student's contextual site evaluation.

In addition to the Integrative Notebook, all M.Div. students are required to submit a two- to three-page reflection paper to their faculty advisors before their hourlong annual evaluation meeting. In these annual reflective papers, the students are asked to reflect upon their learning experiences and struggles and relate them to their formation as ministers.

Given that this new educational approach was adopted only in the fall of 2004, it is too early for the school to see exactly how their students are experiencing and learning from this process. However, there are some early indications of how UTS students are doing in the different areas of integration. Faculty members note that students, on the whole, seem to do fine on the reflection papers on each of the courses they have taken, interacting with themes that surfaced in each course and reflecting upon how they connect with those of other courses. However, when it comes to the annual reflection papers on their own learning experiences, one faculty member noted that there is a good deal of variability in the quality of the reflections the students submit. Perhaps these early observations indicate that while most students are successfully learning how to do cognitive integration, they find personal integration more formidable.

The school is planning to carry out a comprehensive evaluation of its new educational approach in the academic year 2008–2009. Until then, faculty members are using their interactions with their students to gather useful evaluative data. Twice a year, faculty members write reflection papers on their teaching experience as well as what they are hearing from their students; these papers are then discussed during the spring and fall faculty retreats, evaluating how different components of this new approach are working and how their students are learning.

Reflections on United's Approach to Integrative Learning

While the UTS experience of implementing this new approach of learning has been, on the whole, a positive one, it is harder to discern if this approach can work in other seminary settings. To begin, one can argue that the model is more suitable for a smaller school like UTS (it has 149 students in its master's-level programs), a setting in which faculty members know most of the students on campus, not just their own advisees. Also, the amount of time faculty members are required to invest in supervising each student advisee's integrative learning progress limits the size of the advisee group each faculty member can oversee, a condition that many larger schools may not be able to meet (the dean of UTS noted that a full-time faculty member should ideally supervise fifteen or fewer advisees; UTS faculty members currently have around twenty advisees).

Furthermore, because this learning approach's successful outcome is contingent upon all faculty members' full participation in the process and their ability to work as a team, it is paramount that the school attain the entire faculty community's buy-in before implementing the model. For UTS, such faculty support was gained relatively easily partly because its faculty community consisted mostly of new members who were open to new directions and also because it had enjoyed over the years a strong ethos of collective decision-making, a process that involved each faculty member's input. It could have been a much more challenging process had the UTS faculty community been characterized by lack of collaboration, strong attachments to traditional modes of education, or deep political factionalism.

Last, while United's goal is to develop an integrative learning approach that is sensitive to diversity among its students, UTS is not certain if the current model meets this goal. The dean of UTS, acknowledging that the school's faculty and student body lack racial and cultural diversity, is concerned that the new learning approach that is being developed might have some significant cultural blind spots. An Asian American theologian, the only faculty member of non-European heritage, echoes this concern, wondering whether the Indicators for Integration are framed too individualistically, reflecting the cultural ethos of those who come from a European heritage, or that the lack of cultural diversity among faculty members might hinder the school's ability to provide adequate supervision to those students who come from different cultural backgrounds. Do UTS's Indicators of Integration and the process of integrative learning adequately account for cross-cultural and multicultural dynamics? This is a significant question that the UTS community needs to critically explore as it evaluates its new program.

Student Formation: Seeking Personal and Spiritual Wholeness

Closely related to the theme of integration is that of student formation. It is not a coincidence that those schools that are attentive to the issue of integration are also attentive to the process of personal and spiritual formation.[2] Bethel Theological Seminary, also located in St. Paul, Minnesota, is another school that has recently developed new emphases on integration and student formation. This section explores Bethel's approach to formation, focusing particularly on the innovative practices it has developed in helping students overcome and grow through their personal crises.

Bethel Theological Seminary: Being Concerned about Students' Well-Being

In 1995, Bethel Theological Seminary went through a restructuring process, replacing traditional departments with the following three centers: the Center for Biblical and Theological Foundations, the Center for Spiritual and Personal Formation, and the Center for Transformational Leadership. This restructuring process resulted from the school's self-assessment exercise, which indicated that while the school effectively provided its students with a solid biblical and theological foundation, it fell short in meeting the goal of producing graduates who embody high qualities of character and integrity. By establishing the Center for Spiritual and Personal Formation as one of the three centers, the school hoped to better implement its vision to "develop and equip whole and holy persons to serve and lead" churches (Bethel 2006), for as one of the school leaders emphasized, "Healthy pastors lead healthy congregations."

However, in the day-to-day experiences of teaching and learning, the school's strong commitment to the personal and spiritual formation of their students encountered some practical challenges. In Bethel's narrative for The Lexington Seminar (2001), a frustrated fictional faculty member expresses his sentiments in the following way:

> If I start dealing with all those "process things," the students will leave here under-prepared to do the kind of work they're going to be asked to do. Besides, they come here expecting to get a lot of content. Many of them would be frustrated if we started using class time to address everyone's "issues." That's why we have a Student Life Office....In your classes, maybe you can do formation. It's different in the classes in biblical and theological foundations.

During the past several years, Bethel Theological Seminary has sought to develop ways to help the entire seminary community (faculty, staff, and administration) be attentive to the various areas of their students' well-being.

One of the changes Bethel implemented was to replace the Office of Student Life with that of Seminary Student Development, recognizing that traditional student life programming would not help the school provide more robust support for personal formation. The school hired a person with both an M.Div. and an M.A. in counseling to serve as the director of student development. The director works closely with the faculty, equipping them to identify warning signs that students might show and intervene appropriately. Working with other administrators, such as the director of formation and placement and the associate director of personal and professional development, the director of student development formed the Student Development Team and developed intervention plans that encourage students to take appropriate steps toward healing and restoration. Such developmental and intervention plans are typically initiated by the students themselves, although the Student Development Team can initiate the process when a faculty member makes a referral.

Another significant change is the implementation of a quarterly evaluation of students based on careful observation by the Student Development Team and the faculty. The focus of this process is not so much on student evaluation but on providing developmental monitoring and support. Through these processes, the school seeks to identify and assist not only those students who struggle with private issues but to encourage its faculty to be more attentive to all aspects of their students' lives.

As a result of these developments, more seminarians are receiving needed care and support. During the academic year of 2006–2007, the Student Development Team, working closely with faculty, made fifty-four formation interventions, ranging from building a development plan for a student to advising a student to take a year off from seminary education. In Bethel's narrative (2001), a Pastoral Care faculty member made the following appeal:

> We have the best chance to have an impact on our students' formation if it's a coordinated effort—in every classroom, in every required activity, with everyone from staff to administration thinking intentionally about it. If we don't make formation explicit, then we'll never achieve the kind of holistic integration we're hoping for.... We need to change the entire way we do things.

The coordinated effort between the faculty and the Student Development Team in providing student interventions is one concrete action step that indicates that the school is continuing to grow in its commitment to the personal formation of its students.

If it is indeed true that today's students wrestle with many more acute forms of brokenness and fragmentation (Williams 2004, 21–22), their personal and spiritual formation cannot take place in their seminary settings unless it is accompanied by the healing and restoration process. Students often prefer to ignore those issues and patterns that cause them pain or bring them harm, and they often resist any form of intervention because change can be painful. But formation is about change and growth.

Seminaries that are committed to the goal of student formation must be willing to take actions that initially may not be welcomed by their students. Bethel Theological Seminary, during the past several years, has taken critical and intentional steps to develop ways to address its students' personal and spiritual needs, to help them get unstuck so they can continue their journey of formation. For Bethel, being attentive to their students' developmental health is not a small matter because the school believes that it is an indispensable step in achieving its goal of forming healthy pastors who can, in turn, form and lead healthy congregations.

Reflections on Bethel's Approach to Spiritual Formation

As numerous Lexington Seminar school narratives testify, today's seminaries are struggling to find ways to serve their students who bring a wide range of personal problems and issues to their learning community. These issues and problems can be easily perceived as formidable challenges by seminaries; Bethel Theological Seminary sees them as opportunities to form their students. With its commitment to the goal of developing "whole and holy persons to serve and lead," Bethel formed a developmental and interventional approach to care for its students. This pastoral model of student formation, as appealing and admirable as it may be, nonetheless faces a number of constant, resistant forces within the seminary setting that can undermine its sustainability and effectiveness.

In many ways, seminary is not a place that promotes self-disclosure, a place where students can easily reveal their own struggles and pain. As an academic institution, seminary expects its students to perform their best and attain the best possible grade; it is a place that values personal excellence and achievement. Similarly, as a place of ministry preparation, seminary is also a setting in which students are expected to demonstrate their fitness for ministry; it is a place that encourages students to present the best part of themselves to the public. Yet Bethel's approach to personal and spiritual formation invites students to reveal their worst part to others, those areas of their lives that need healing and growth. The effectiveness of the model, thus, is contingent upon students' willingness to go against the ethos of most seminaries. Given this challenge, a successful implementation of an intervention-oriented student formation model requires also a formation of the school's institutional culture that would intentionally deepen the level of trust among the faculty, staff, and students and would strongly promote values of authenticity, vulnerability, and healing.

Furthermore, Bethel's approach to student formation calls for a deep institutional commitment, because its approach can compete with the other interests of the school. For instance, as one Bethel faculty member noted, the school's commitment to student formation can conflict with the school's enrollment and retention goals. The enrollment office often contacts and encourages those students who are on probation to return to campus, although such an action goes against the recommendation offered by the school's Student Development Team. In other cases, students who seek to follow the recommendation and take some time off from seminary training face formidable new challenges because they lose housing and financial aid for that year. These and other institutional and personal costs make this formation approach a difficult option for those seminaries that are financially strapped. For others, these practical implications invite them to carefully count the cost of serving their students who have many needs.

An Artistic Model for Today's Theological Education

The above three seminaries' experiences demonstrate clearly that the task of addressing the issue of student learning and formation, particularly in today's context of increasing student diversity, calls for significant change in the way faculty envision and practice their own vocational teaching in theological education. Yet, like other institutionalized communities, seminaries and their faculties are often reluctant to embrace change even as they acknowledge its necessity. How does a dean, then, invite and motivate faculty colleagues to collaborate in such changes? Furthermore, how does a dean, working with faculty, begin to change the culture of an institution to achieve optimal results for student learning and formation? Finally, to foster such a collaborative partnership with the faculty, what are some initiatives a dean can employ in the area of faculty development, both individually and corporately? To address these and other related questions, I would like to propose a model/paradigm of faculty engagement (see Figure 2.1), an approach that, I hope, will generate constructive conversations about substantial issues that face today's seminaries.

Theatrical Improvisation: The Skill of Disciplined Spontaneity

In today's world of constant, rapid, and complex changes, business schools and corporations acknowledge that they need to develop a new model of management and leadership, one that will enable them to respond more effectively to their ever-changing business environments. A growing number of these institutions are turning to artists to learn how to reconceptualize their understanding of management and leadership (Adler 2006), and many corporate organizations are exploring improvisation as one of the artistic processes that can help them to learn the skills of "disciplined spontaneity."[3] The assumption here is that traditional methods of long-term planning may not serve the group well. Instead, the organization needs to learn to blend the skills of planning with the ability to respond to new opportunities and challenges in a timely and creative manner.

So why should a seminary faculty community explore improvisation as a potential source of inspiration and insight as it wrestles with the theme of student learning and formation? At first glance, the use of improvisation may seem out of step with a seminary's educational process and its way of doing things. However, as Donald Schön has demonstrated, one of the goals of the training of professional practitioners—such as doctors, lawyers, or engineers—should be to help them develop the ability to do "reflection-in-action," to learn how to improvise reflectively in their professional practice (Schön 1983, 1987). In *Educating Clergy*, Foster and colleagues make a similar claim about theological education, about the training of clergy. Assuming that one of the main aims of theological education is to enable seminarians to nurture a "pastoral imagination," Foster and colleagues argue that it is important for seminary faculty members to model before their students "pedagogical imagination," a process that involves, among other things, one's ability to improvise in teaching (Foster et al. 2006, 59–64). Indeed, Foster and his team of researchers found that effective seminary faculty members are those who improvise effectively in their teaching:

> We interviewed and observed highly skilled teachers. They were almost intuitively adept at making technical pedagogical decisions on the spot to shift the focus of the conversation, to introduce new information, to pick up the pace of session, to alter the plans for the session, to defuse distractions and refocus discussion. (Foster et al. 2006, 62)

The art of improvisation, in short, is not as removed from the task of teaching as some may think.

Seminaries should consider improvisation as a tool for faculty engagement because of its potential value in addressing the issue of student learning and diversity. Given the reality of rapidly changing and diversifying student populations, seminaries are coming to recognize the need for different ways of teaching and learning (such as disciplined spontaneity), not just a tinkering of the current system. The art of improvisation can help faculty members develop the ability to respond reflexively and effectively to ever-changing student body profiles. Second, the issue of student diversity often generates conversations of identity politics that can be divisive, potentially hindering faculty and administrators from working together to find new ways to offer a theological education that might benefit all students. By employing an artistic process such as improvisation, the

Figure 2.1: Theatrical Improvisation Model: A New Vision of Student Learning and Formation in Today's Diverse Student World.

Goal: Assist faculty in discerning the complex and changing student community and in thinking creatively about student learning and formation.

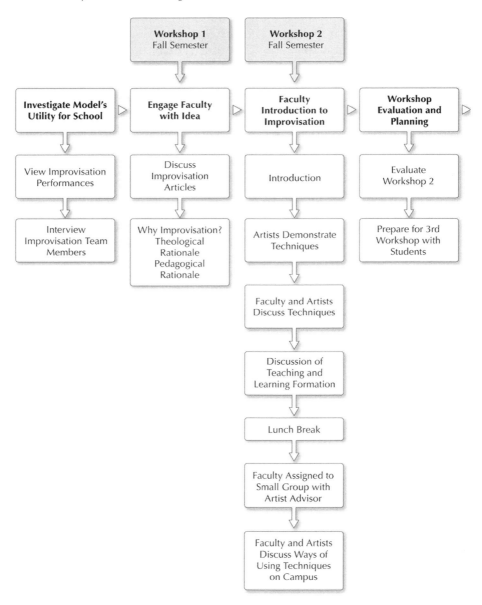

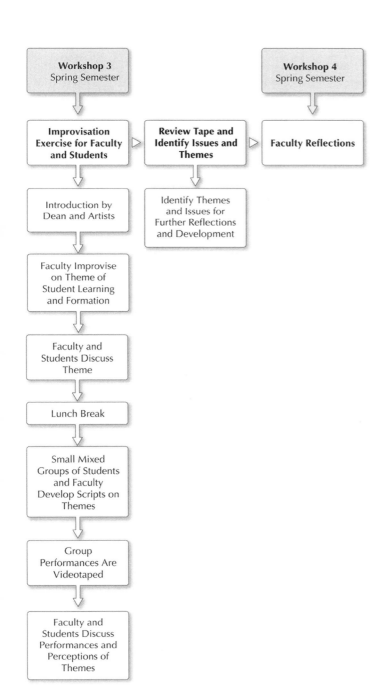

school is creating a new and even an unfamiliar liminal space for its faculty conversations, a kind of space that can encourage the faculty community to be creative and imaginative in approaching the issue of student learning and formation.

Finally, and perhaps most significantly, this approach has the potential to promote change in faculty culture that might, in turn, contribute positively to the faculty community's ability to engage other significant and complex issues their school might be facing. Recently, several theologians fruitfully explored drama, particularly theatrical improvisation, as a model of doing theology in today's world (see Wells 2004; Vanhoozer 2005). In their view, theatrical improvisation is an appropriate model for Christian faith and Christian community because it, among other things, can deepen our understanding of and commitment to (1) others in the faith community, (2) the larger redemptive story that is unfolding, a purposeful narrative in which everyone plays a part, and (3) the Christian formation of individuals and their communities.

Community of Attentiveness and Trust

Theatrical improvisation is often misunderstood as an unscripted and off-the-cuff performance of clever individuals. Instead, it is an art that requires disciplined attentiveness to others, as each performer's next line and acting are greatly dependent upon what others are saying and doing. Furthermore, improvisation calls for deep mutual trust among the performers; the performance breaks down when performers follow a script without responding to the behavior of others. Instead, when a team of performers learns to trust and cooperate with one another and achieve a state of genuine, creative harmony, performers and the audience can both experience the fascination and joy of improvisation.

Today's seminaries, like other institutions of higher education, are often characterized by various expressions of individualism, where teaching and learning are pursued as isolated, individualistic activities. Having been trained in doctoral programs in research-based universities, many seminary faculty members had been socialized to view themselves as independent contractors, focusing only on one's courses and research projects and failing to be attentive to the activities and experiences of other members of the learning community. Such an ethos greatly hinders an academic community's ability to respond collectively to the various challenges it faces, including its ability to address the changing profile and needs of its students. The art of improvisation challenges seminary communities to recognize the critical importance of being attentive to the voices and actions of other constituents of the school community, including those of students. When a seminary's faculty begin to be attentive to one another, as Claremont's faculty is doing through its practice of systematic listening, such an intentional practice can gradually change the culture of the institution, enabling it to respond to rising needs more aptly.

Improvisation also teaches seminary faculty members to see their learning community as a community of trust. For improvising performers, trust is not merely an abstract idea; in order for them to improvise, they must trust that their colleagues are fully engaged with the entire ensemble and not focusing exclusively on their own needs. As schools face increasing diversity, the task of building a community that is characterized by attentiveness and trust is especially critical—but also increasingly challenging. What might be some lessons we can learn in these areas from improvisational performers, their training, and their performances?

Community of Shared Stories

Malcolm Warford, director of The Lexington Seminar, once observed in a consultation gathering that many seminaries' response to increasing student diversity is simply to enlarge the educational "container" in which they place a wider range of cultural perspectives, practices, and histories. The limitation of this model, Warford points out, is that it may enable schools to bring together in one place students from diverse backgrounds, but it does not help students learn how to relate to one another in a meaningful, integrative way. Furthermore, such a model, by trying to be all things to all people, can contribute to the diffusion, if not loss, of each school's unique sense of vision and calling.

While improvisational performers exercise a degree of freedom in improvising, they, compared to other actors and actresses who participate in a scripted drama, must have an even deeper understanding of the story to keep the narrative going. This deepened understanding of the shared narrative is another critical factor that contributes to the creative harmony in an improvisational performance. Each seminary, as a learning and faith community, has many stories that have shaped and are continually shaping the institution. What is the particular vision of the school that formed and sustained its educational ministry thus far? What are theological traditions that inform the school's identity and mission? And, finally, as a Christian community, how does the school participate in the larger story of the gospel as the school learns to be attentive to the leading of God's Spirit and in God's call to be faithful to the gospel of Jesus Christ? An alternative to the container model of diversity, then, is to lift up those purposeful narratives that can invite and unite all members of the seminary community—playing different roles and in different scenes—but keeping the same narrative going with a shared understanding and goal. Increasing diversity, therefore, might mean that the school leadership needs to focus *more* on the unique mission and identity of the school and learn to tell and live out those stories that have shaped the school with *more* conviction, not *less*.

Community of Formation and Integration

The art of improvisation requires years of disciplined preparation from its performers, requiring not only acting skills but also an ability to be alert, adaptive, discerning, and courageous in facing the unknown.[4] The goal of the training is to help the performer to be one with the whole context: self, other performers, the story, and audience. It is understandable that Aristotle employed the metaphor of theatrical improvisation to describe the workings of practical wisdom (Nussbaum 1990, 37). The goal and the process of training improvisers are similar to the integrative and formational learning this paper has emphasized for today's theological education, a kind of learning that prepares students to serve effectively in today's diverse and rapidly changing contexts of ministry. United Theological Seminary's implementation of new integrative learning, in many ways, demonstrates how one seminary is working toward this goal.

Improvisation as a Way of Faculty Development

For the reasons mentioned above, the improvisational arts can be a useful and potent resource for engaging seminary faculty members. A recent experience at the 2007 annual conference of the Religious Education Association (REA) bears wonderful testament to this potential. During the conference, a Boston-based improvisational group called the True Story Theater was invited to perform and interact with the audience on the theme of intercultural dynamics. Mary Hess, an associate professor of religious education at Luther Seminary and one of the participants in The Lexington Seminar's Academic Mentoring Program, experienced this event and made the following observations:

> The group had us laughing, sighing with pain, wondering, pondering...and the audience was all professors....The group had a great touch for inviting us into the process, but they did it in a way that allowed people to enter at their own pace....I can easily imagine a seminary inviting this group in to do one session and then using that as a springboard for further faculty work.

If so, how might a dean use this rich resource to help faculty see their roles in a different way and be open to the larger project of bringing change to the culture of the faculty and of the larger seminary community? The final sections of this essay offer a seven-step design through which a dean might begin such a process of collaboration and change.

1. Investigating the Model's Utility for the School

During the summer, the dean begins the process by forming a steering committee that consists of faculty members who represent different academic and personal backgrounds. With this committee, the dean begins learning about theatrical improvisation and investigating the potential utility of this approach of engaging the faculty (see the selected bibliography listed in the appendix following this essay), and when the group is ready to take the next step, it can begin the process of identifying an appropriate local or regional team of professional improvisers. Currently, there are many improvisation teams (often called forum theater groups or applied improvisation artists) that have some interactions with business or educational institutions (visit www.appliedimprov.net/blog/people for more information). Once a potential group is identified, the team should view the group's performance and interview some members of the performing team to see if they would be interested in entering into a dialogue with the seminary faculty.

Having had an opportunity to explore and experience theatrical improvisation, the steering group should then seek to identify not only the strengths and limitations of this approach but also any potential resistance it might encounter and find ways to invite the rest of the community to participate in this process. If the approach of improvisation is to be effective in helping faculty members think creatively about the activities of teaching and learning and thus play a significant role in creating a new institutional culture, faculty buy-in is imperative. Different schools, given their own unique institutional culture and the profile of the faculty community, might encounter different forms of resistance; thus, in the end, the dean of each school must seek to find and develop its own way of managing potential resistance and in implementing the approach proposed in this paper. In a sense, the process of recruiting faculty to be engaged in a creative process like improvisation also requires the dean to exercise a certain level of creativity—to practice both pastoral and pedagogical imaginations.

2. Engaging Faculty with the Idea: Fall Faculty Workshop 1 (Half Day)

At the beginning of fall semester, the dean and the faculty steering committee lead a half-day faculty workshop in which they introduce the theatrical improvisation model as a form of faculty engagement and to highlight some of its potential benefits. In doing so, the process can involve the following three steps:

1. Prior to the workshop, the steering committee distributes selected reading materials (such as Moshavi's "Yes and… " [2001], Yanow's "Learning in and from Improvising" [2001], and Adler's "Arts and Leadership" [2006]) and asks faculty members to prepare to explore the question, "Why improvisation?"

2. At the workshop gathering, the dean invites an improvisation artist to describe how this particular form of art can enrich an educational process of teaching and learning. At this point, it may even be a good idea to invite a theological educator who has experienced applied improvisation (such as someone who attended the 2007 REA annual conference and had an opportunity to experience the performance of the True Story Theater) and ask that educator to discuss the value of the experience.

3. The dean and the steering committee lead small group discussions, giving faculty members a chance to process their thoughts and feelings as they evaluate this less-than-familiar approach to faculty engagement.

If there is much resistance from the faculty, perhaps the dean can first introduce other, perhaps less edgy, art forms to the faculty community, to help the faculty community see the potential value of the arts in learning to see things differently. For instance, the faculty community can view and discuss a short documentary film called *Sketches of Frank Gehry* (2005), in which Sidney Pollack interviews the renowned architect, exploring the different ways in which Gehry seeks to expand his way of seeing and designing things. Perhaps it might make it easier for some faculty members to have such an experience first before experiencing improvisational theater, which can seem too subjective and radical.

If the faculty community is open to the idea of learning from improvisational arts but finds improvisational acting too edgy, perhaps the dean can introduce other forms of improvisation that feel safer to faculty members. The faculty community can, for instance, try out an exercise called "improvisational storytelling" (see Appendix B for a description and instructions), an exercise that is designed to involve all participants at a level of minimal risk taking. Or the faculty community can start the process by attempting a mid-level (in terms of risk taking) improvisational exercise and try out the "statues" exercise (see Appendix C), an exercise that might make some feel more vulnerable than improvisational storytelling but not as much as improvisational acting. In short, there are many different types and levels of improvisational exercises that the dean can utilize, depending on the degree of openness of a given faculty community.

3. Improvisation Performance and Dialogue: Fall Faculty Workshop 2 (Full Day)

Once the faculty has decided to explore more fully this model of faculty engagement and the steering committee has identified a suitable team of improvisation consultants, the dean should then schedule a full-day faculty workshop later in the fall semester, inviting all faculty members. As the workshop begins, the dean should explain briefly the purpose of the gathering and introduce the improvisational team. As the artists prepare to offer a thirty-minute performance on a theme that relates to student learning or student diversity, the dean encourages faculty members to be attentive to the specific ways the actors improvise and imagine how their own activities as faculty members are similar to (or different from) the performance they are observing. The performance is then followed by a discussion session which begins with the performers explaining various aspects of their training and performance followed by a larger discussion of how improvisation relates to the task of teaching and learning in seminary.

After an extended lunch period during which faculty members have an opportunity to mingle with the artists, the dean begins the afternoon session by assigning faculty members to small groups. Each group, which includes one or two improvisers who serve as consultants, then focuses on a specific issue that relates to student learning and formation. With the help of the performers, each group has an opportunity to improvise on a given issue, giving faculty members a chance to see how this practice has relevance for thinking from different angles on common, shared knowledge. (See Appendix D for an improvisational acting exercise recently developed by a group of theologians.)

The faculty workshop then concludes with a session in which the faculty and the artists come together as one group and think about ways in which the faculty and the rest of the seminary community can intentionally create space in classrooms and campus life where the dynamics of improvisation can be experienced more fully. Perhaps faculty members can think about ways to develop and practice different teaching methods that are particularly attentive to the needs of different students, methods that encourage faculty members to actively listen to their students as they prepare and present their teaching curriculum. Perhaps the chapel worship service can be identified as a time when the whole community, including the faculty, can "perform" their different roles in the divine story of salvation and redemption. Perhaps the dean and a group of faculty can start the process of identifying and "performing" a set of stories that can inform and shape the seminary community and deepen its understanding of mission and calling. In short, this exercise, and the rest of the workshop experience, seeks to inspire the imagination of the faculty community in such a way that it begins to embrace a set of new values and practices and a new way of seeing.

4. Workshop Evaluation and Planning

After the faculty workshop, the dean meets with a group of faculty members to evaluate the experience and its impact. This evaluative process has two main goals: (1) find ways to follow up on ideas that emerged from the workshop experience, thus continuing conversations that surfaced and thinking about ways to implement specific practices; (2) evaluate the effectiveness of an improvisational approach in the faculty workshop. What elements were particularly helpful and what elements can be further improved? These evaluative reflections help the faculty group design the next phase of the process, namely offering another improvisation workshop, this time involving the faculty and a select group of students.

5. Improvisation with Students: Spring Faculty Workshop 1 (Full Day)

One of the main goals of this workshop in the spring semester is to help the faculty community to learn more about the generation of students they are teaching, particularly about their learning and formation experiences. Before the workshop, the dean and a faculty group carefully select a group of students who reflect the diversity of the student body and invite them to participate in the upcoming workshop. The number of students should roughly equal that of the faculty.

On the day of the workshop, the dean or a faculty member can open the day's event by explaining what improvisation is and why it might be a helpful metaphor for the seminary community as it reflects on its mission and educational process. A professional improvisation artist then offers a brief introduction to improvisation performance, particularly for the benefit of students. Then a group of faculty members improvise on a theme that relates to teaching and learning on campus, followed by a discussion on how this particular group of faculty members perceived and scripted how students experience their theological education.

In the afternoon, each small group, consisting of faculty and students, is given an issue that relates to some critical area of student learning and formation in today's theological education. Some groups might focus on the issue of teaching and learning in classroom settings, while others might focus on the issue of spiritual formation or personal crisis that require the school's intervention (as Bethel's case study illustrated), and each group prepares a short script to be improvised. This time, however, faculty and students work collaboratively on the script. Particular care should be given to assure that students' concerns and experiences are adequately reflected in the narrative.

Finally, each group has an opportunity to offer a ten- to fifteen-minute-long improvisation (not everyone in the small group needs to participate in the performance), and each group's performance is videotaped. After every group has performed, the entire group comes together to reflect on what they have seen and heard and evaluate what they experienced during the day.

6. Identifying Issues and Themes: An Ethnographic Study

After the workshop, the faculty steering committee and a small group of students who participated in the improvisational experience meet to review and analyze the videotapes that recorded each group's performance. Through this process, the group aims to identify certain issues and concerns that have emerged as well as the ways in which different groups sought to respond to these challenges and opportunities. Finally, the group analyzes the insights gained about the current generation of students and the implications for the school's task of student learning and formation.

7. Faculty Reflections and Evaluation: Spring Faculty Workshop 2 (Half Day)

Toward the end of the spring semester, the dean convenes a half-day faculty workshop in which the faculty community has an opportunity to hear the report from the study group mentioned above. Using the report as a stepping-stone, the faculty body then engages in a series of conversations that focus on the areas of student diversity and student learning and formation in the seminary, evaluating current experiences and envisioning new approaches to explore. Finally, if this experience is found helpful, the faculty community can explore the possibility of having a faculty-student improvisation workshop once every three years, enabling faculty members to hear and experience the particular needs and concerns that different generations of students bring to their classrooms and their campus community.

Conclusion

As the student population becomes increasingly diverse, one of the foundational tasks today's seminaries face is to know who their students are. The improvisation model presented in this chapter aims to create a space in which faculty members can listen to their students—and to one another—in a particular way. Rather than offering yet another round of analysis of and discussion about the issue of student diversity, this model invites faculty members to experience new realities that are being created on their campuses, those unexpected happenings and situations that emerge in part due to student diversity. As they grow in their ability to listen attentively to their students' voices and observe appreciatively new experiences their diverse students bring to their campus community, it is my hope that faculty members will also grow in their ability to exercise "disciplined spontaneity," enabling them to be faithful to their vocational calling as theological educators in today's rapidly changing educational setting.

Appendix A

Selected Bibliography on Improvisation

Adler, Nancy. 2006. "The Arts and Leadership: Now That We Can Do Anything, What Will We Do?" *Academy of Management Learning and Education* 5 (4): 486–499.

Merry, Tim. 2003. "Statues." In *Orchestrating Collaboration at Work: Using Music, Improvisation, Storytelling, and Other Arts to Improve Teamwork,* edited by A. VanGundy and L. Naiman. San Francisco: Jossey-Bass.

Moshavi, Dan. 2001. " 'Yes and…': Introducing Improvisational Theatre Techniques to the Management Classroom." *Journal of Management Education* 25 (4): 437–449.

Nissley, Nick. 2003. "Fictionalization and Imaginative Restoryation: Storytelling Techniques to Enhance Organizational Effectiveness." In *Orchestrating Collaboration at Work: Using Music, Improvisation, Storytelling, and Other Arts to Improve Teamwork,* edited by A. VanGundy and L. Naiman. San Francisco: Jossey-Bass.

———, Steven Taylor, and Linda Houden. 2004. "The Politics of Performance in Organizational Theatre-based Training and Interventions." *Organization Studies* 25(5): 817–839.

Wells, Samuel. 2004. *Improvisation: The Drama of Christian Ethics.* Grand Rapids: Brazos Press.

VanGundy, A., and L. Naiman, eds. 2003. *Orchestrating Collaboration at Work: Using Music, Improvisation, Storytelling, and Other Arts to Improve Teamwork.* San Francisco: Jossey-Bass.

Yanow, Dvera. 2001. "Learning in and from Improvising: Lessons from Theatre for Organizational Learning." *Reflections* 4 (2): 58–62.

Appendix B

Improvisational Story Telling[5]

- Set up the exercise by posting different images (150–200) on the wall.
- Invite the participants to individually select an image that "speaks to them" about the question under discussion. For example, the participants may be asked to think about a time when they felt more alive than usual because of the diversity in their classroom.
- Choose a partner.
- To one's partner each participant describes the image one has chosen and makes a connection between the image and the question, telling the story (three to five minutes).
- The partner, the listener, describes what he or she sees in the image and makes his or her own connections from the presenter's image.
- The partner asks questions and explores meanings, searching for insights (not problem solving, prescribing, or imposing judgment).
- Finally, the storyteller thanks the other (tellers are the final author of the meaning of the image they chose).

- Then presenters and listeners switch roles. The listener becomes the teller and vice versa. Repeat the above steps of telling and listening.
- After the one-on-one, partnered sharing (which is the starting place, offering the safety of talking with just one other person), break the group into groups of eight or ten. In each story sharing circle, each individual has the opportunity to share an encapsulated story prompted by one's chosen image (essentially recounting what was shared earlier with a partner). After each person has shared a story, the facilitator asks a set of group processing questions. For example, the facilitator might ask, What threads were common in all of these stories?
- A part two, if time permits, can be used to ask individuals to find an image that speaks to what they would do differently to more effectively embrace diversity in their teaching and then repeat the above steps. This allows for "restoryation"—a notion from narrative therapy that affords participants a vehicle to create more functional storylines and try them on.

Appendix C

Statues: Improvisational Sculpting of Group Dynamics[6]
(Adapted from Boal's Theatre of the Oppressed)

- Set up the exercise by explaining that it affords participants an opportunity to move out of their "heads" and into their "bodies," to improvisationally sculpt group dynamics, using ourselves as the clay.
- With the assistance of a volunteer, the facilitator role models for the participants how they, the sculptors, can make statues. Sculpt the volunteer by moving parts of his or her body (such as hands, arms, and legs) into a desired shape or position. This is done in silence and without showing the person how to be but by physically moving parts of the body.
- The facilitator explains that larger, more complex statues can be created by modeling many individuals. For example, two people shaking hands can symbolize a greeting, or three people pointing skyward might be watching shooting stars.
- To get started, the facilitator asks a volunteer to act as the sculptor. Ask the volunteer to make a sculpture that represents the question the group is seeking to answer. For example, the question might be, What does this conflict feel like and why is it so difficult to resolve? The sculptor should select, in silence, three to five individuals from

the larger group to be the clay for sculpting. Silently, the sculptor begins his or her work.

- After the statue is built, invite the audience to reflect upon the image and perhaps journal some thoughts and feelings. The facilitator can speak to the image and pose questions. The facilitator can also invite others from the larger group to alter the statue and change it into something else, based on the facilitated conversation. For example, If you had spent time upfront getting to know one another, how might that have led to a different outcome?

- A facilitated dialogue amongst the entire group should focus on what they see in the statue. The facilitator can talk to the statue and allow it to mediate the dialogue. The facilitator can address any individual in the sculpture and ask the audience, "What do you think he or she might be feeling or thinking?" This helps deepen the understanding of the group dynamics.

- To conclude, ask the participants to sculpt an ideal situation, thus affording an element of restoryation for creating new, more idealized futures.

Appendix D

Developing An Improvisational Scenario[7]

- Hand out 5x8 blank cards to all participants.
- Announce the overall theme for the session—for example: the gift and challenge of intercultural communication. It should be something specific but open to multiple interpretations.
- Ask participants to write on their 5x8 cards an experience or scene that comes to mind for them as illustrative of that theme.
- Ask participants to lay their 5x8 cards on the floor in the center of the room. If one participant's scene is similar to another's, that person should place his or her card close by. If it is not similar, that person should place it apart.
- Once all participants have laid down their cards, take a moment to group them into a number of clusters that would match a good number of groups, based roughly on dividing the whole group into smaller groups of from six to eight people.
- Explain the rules: (1) Be concrete in developing a scene. (2) Make sure there is a title for the scene. (3) Name the roles people are playing. (4) Do not rehearse the scene (other than perhaps blocking out the props needed for the scene and the approximate movement of participants).

- Ask participants to choose the cluster they want to work with.
- Have groups go off and work out their scenes (allowing roughly forty-five minutes to do this).
- When all of the groups are back, have each group enact its scene in the front of the room. After each scene, the facilitator asks, first, what members of the group felt while they were performing, and then, what the audience felt about it.
- After this has been done for each of the group scenes, the facilitator closes this segment by facilitating a short discussion of the insights that have emerged from the process overall.

Notes

1. Initially they were called "benchmarks"; however, the faculty decided to use the term "indicators" because it is a more dynamic term that implies that diverse students would evidence integration in different ways.
2. The term "formation" has a range of meanings in different ecclesiastical contexts. While Roman Catholic seminaries use the term to refer to the entire program of priestly development, thus highlighting academic, pastoral, spiritual, and human formation as the four foundational elements of their programs, Protestant seminaries, including The Lexington Seminar schools, tend to use the term "formation" to refer to the latter two elements: spiritual and personal formation.
3. While this proposal focuses on improvisation, various organizations have studied and used other theater approaches. For a helpful study that examines and assesses these approaches, see Nissley, Taylor, and Houden (2004).
4. Educators often employ role play as a teaching tool. It is important to distinguish improvisation from role play. While role play may employ certain improvisation skills, it requires less imagination and creativity since those who participate in the roles know well the context and the situation. In a role play, the person who leads it also gives definition to the context and its expectations. Theatrical improvisation, on the other hand, involves a group of individuals who are asked to represent a fully new situation in which context and intention are less known and predictable.
5. Adapted from Nissley (2003, 199–202).
6. Adapted from Merry (2003, 257–259).
7. These directions are drawn from a process used at the conference, The Gift and Challenge of Intercultural Communication, Fordham University, February 2008. The process is based in part on—and works specifically within—a communicative theology framework. For more on communicative theology, see Sharer and Hilberath (2008) and Forschungskreis Kommunikative Theologie [Communicative Theology Research Group] (2007).

References

Adler, Nancy. 2006. "The Arts and Leadership: Now That We Can Do Anything, What Will We Do?" *Academy of Management Learning and Education* 5 (4): 486–499.

Association of Theological Schools of the United States and Canada. 2003. *Fact Book on Theological Education, 2002–2003*. Pittsburgh, PA: Association of Theological Schools.

Austin Presbyterian Theological Seminary. 1999. Project Narrative. http://www.lexingtonseminar.org/archive/archive_doc.php/doctype/narrative/id/259/

Bethel Theological Seminary. 2001. Project Narrative. http://www.lexingtonseminar.org/archive/archive_doc.php/doctype/narrative/id/271/

———. 2006. Vision Statement. http://seminary.bethel.edu/catalog/profile/vision.html.

Brookfield, Stephen D. 1986. *Understanding and Facilitating Adult Learning*. San Francisco: Jossey-Bass.

Church Divinity School of the Pacific. 2001. Project Narrative. http://www.lexingtonseminar.org/archive/archive_doc.php/doctype/narrative/id/272/

Claremont School of Theology. 2000. Project Report. http://www.lexingtonseminar.org/archive/archive_doc.php/doctype/report/id/266/

Dykstra, C. R. 2001. "The Pastoral Imagination," *Initiatives in Religion* 9 (1): 1–11.

Forschungskreis Kommunikative Theologie [Communicative Theology Research Group]. 2007. *Kommunikative Theologie: Selbstvergwisserung unserer Kultur des Theologietreibens [Communicative Theology: Reflections on the Culture of our Practice of Theology]*. Wien: Lit Verlag.

Foster, Charles R. 2002. "Diversity in Theological Education." *Theological Education* 38 (2): 15–38.

———, Lisa Dahill, Larry Golemon, and Barbara Wang Tolentino. 2006. *Educating Clergy: Teaching Practices and Pastoral Imagination*. San Francisco: Jossey-Bass.

Klimoski, Victor, Kevin O'Neil, and Katarina Schuth. 2005. *Educating Leaders for Ministry*. Collegeville, MN: Liturgical Press.

Merriam, Sharan, and Rosemary Caffarella. 1999. *Learning in Adulthood: A Comprehensive Guide*. San Francisco: Jossey-Bass.

Merry, Tim. 2003. "Statues." In *Orchestrating Collaboration at Work: Using Music, Improvisation, Storytelling, and Other Arts to Improve Teamwork*, edited by A. VanGundy and L. Naiman. San Francisco: Jossey-Bass.

Moshavi, Dan. 2001. "'Yes and...': Introducing Improvisational Theatre Techniques to the Management Classroom." *Journal of Management Education* 25 (4): 437–449.

Nissley, Nick. 2003. "Fictionalization and Imaginative Restoryation: Storytelling Techniques to Enhance Organizational Effectiveness." In *Orchestrating Collaboration at Work: Using Music, Improvisation, Storytelling, and Other Arts to Improve Teamwork*, edited by A. VanGundy and L. Naiman. San Francisco: Jossey-Bass.

———, Steven Taylor, and Linda Houden. 2004. "The Politics of Performance in Organizational Theatre-based Training and Interventions." *Organization Studies* 25 (5): 817–839.

Nussbaum, Martha C. 1990. *Love's Knowledge: Essays on Philosophy and Literature*. New York: Oxford University Press.

Pollack, Sidney, dir. 2005. *Sketches of Frank Gehry*. American Masters.

Scharer, Matthias, and Bernd Jochen Hilberath. 2008. *The Practice of Communicative Theology* (New York: Crossroad Publishing Company.

Schön, Donald A. 1983. *The Reflective Practitioner: How Professionals Think in Action*. New York: Basic Books.

———. 1987. *Educating the Reflective Practitioner: Toward a New Design for Teaching and Learning in the Professions*. San Francisco: Jossey-Bass.

Siew, Yau Man, and Gary Peluso-Verdend. 2005. "Interpreting Protestant Student Voices." *Theological Education* 40 (2): 47–64.

United Theological Seminary of the Twin Cities. 2002. *Indicators of Integration.* Transcript.

———. 2001a. Project Narrative. http://www.lexingtonseminar.org/archive/archive_ doc.php/doctype/narrative/id/275/

———. 2001b. Project Report. http://www.lexingtonseminar.org/archive/archive_doc. php/doctype/report/id/275/

VanGundy, A., and L. Naiman, eds. 2003. *Orchestrating Collaboration at Work: Using Music, Improvisation, Storytelling, and Other Arts to Improve Teamwork.* San Francisco: Jossey-Bass.

Vanhoozer, Kevin. 2005. *The Drama of Doctrine: A Canonical Linguistic Approach to Christian Theology.* Louisville, KY: Westminster John Knox Press.

Wells, Samuel. 2004. *Improvisation: The Drama of Christian Ethics.* Grand Rapids: Brazos Press.

Williams, Raymond. 2004. "The Vocation of Teaching: Beyond the Conspiracy of Mediocrity." In *Practical Wisdom: On Theological Teaching and Learning,* ed. Malcolm L. Warford, 15–28. New York: Peter Lang Publishing.

Winkelmes, Mary-Ann. 2005. "Formative Learning in the Classroom." In *Practical Wisdom: On Theological Teaching and Learning,* ed. Malcolm L. Warford, 161–179. New York: Peter Lang Publishing.

Yanow, Dvera. 2001. "Learning in and from Improvising: Lessons from Theatre for Organizational Learning." *Reflections* 4 (2): 58–62.

3. Listening and Learning to Teach in Theological Contexts: An Appreciative Inquiry Model

MARY E. HESS

A central dilemma facing theological education is the fundamental mismatch between the process by which most faculty earn a Ph.D. in theological fields and the skills required to be an effective teacher, especially given the diverse characteristics of today's students.

The Challenges We Face: Learning to Support Learning

For most faculty, achieving a Ph.D. is a process that entails long hours of individual study, intermittently broken by intense discussion in seminars or meetings with a dissertation advisor. Successfully navigating a dissertation, getting a paper accepted into a scholarly conference, or publishing in a journal are all tasks that demand the ability to be self-directed, focused, intent on critical inquiry, and an effective writer. These capacities are crucial in supporting learning more generally, but they are not enough, in and of themselves, for effectively teaching today's diverse student population.

Mary Boys has written, "Religious education is the making accessible of the traditions of the religious community and the making manifest of the intrinsic connection between traditions and transformation" (1989, 193). This is an excellent definition for the narrower field of theological education, and it points directly at our challenge, because "making accessible" and "making manifest" are not processes much observed in doctoral education as currently construed.

In order to make something accessible—whether that is the tradition of biblical study in an original language, the practice of understanding liturgical rubrics, or the method of historical study—faculty must be able to discern what students know about a topic and be able to design a variety of tasks that make access to the topic not only possible but inviting enough to engage students. In other words, faculty must be able to diagnose student needs and prescribe appropriate interventions to meet them.

Making something manifest goes a step further, particularly in Boys's use of the phrase through which she seeks to connect tradition to transformation. To make something manifest is to bring something to life in another's understanding. Indeed, in our context it is an invitation not only to participate in the tradition actively but to lead within it. Such an invitation inevitably transforms the teacher, as well as the student—and transforms the tradition under study.

Making the tradition accessible and manifest for today's students and today's environment, which is one of continual change, necessitates continual learning. It is no longer sufficient for faculty to master a field of study and have the requisite skills to pass such mastery onto students. Faculty must also learn how to learn and to do so in the midst of institutions that are facing some of the most stressful and difficult circumstances seminaries have had to face in decades.

Because the challenges are so great and because they strike at the heart of their chosen vocation, seminary professors need spaces of profound respect and trust in which to collaboratively seek answers to the question: "Is it possible I could prepare for all these years only to discover that what I have been prepared for is not what my job consists of?" The Lexington Seminar has created one such place in which faculty fears and dilemmas can be voiced within a surround that is supportive enough that doubts can emerge as interesting questions rather than ego-threatening challenges. It is not surprising that most of the schools that have participated in The Lexington Seminar have tried to find ways to duplicate its process in their home contexts. Many of these schools now recognize how important the gifts of time and space are, not only for faculty but for students as well.

Indeed, there are strong similarities between the questions seminary professors are asking and the questions their students are asking. The mismatch between faculty preparation and the actual tasks of seminary professors exists in part because seminary students do not look like, act like, think like, or even feel like the seminary students of fifty years ago.

If today's seminary students had been as deeply socialized into a specific community of faith, if they had come from the same educational background, the same moment in their life journey, and the same (or similar) class backgrounds as their professors, then seminary professors could take for granted basic catechetical preparation and delve immediately into the kinds of questions they, themselves, studied as graduate students. They could invite their students into complex discussions of abstract points, ask them to enter the conversation at the same place, and invite them into theological research. Indeed, this is why doctoral-level education still tends to work as well as it does: most doctoral students share at least some of the key characteristics of their professors.

But seminary students do *not* come from similar backgrounds. They do *not* share the same formation, the same moment in their life journey, the same ability to maneuver among abstract conceptualizations. They are, for the most part, involved in a different conversation that has taught them to use different tools. They come to seminary interested in active leadership outside of the academy, and they arrive at seminary sometimes unprepared for the educational processes that await them there. Most, if not all, students find themselves in a crisis of identity early in their seminary time. They wonder, "Should I really be at seminary? Why am I here? What will sustain me in the coming years? How can I know that what the seminary offers to teach me is really what I need to know?"

Students who have had previous professional experiences are often able to live into this uncertainty with a particular kind of patience. They know they have endured such not-knowing in the past, and they believe they will come through it again. Whatever sustained them previously often becomes their coping mechanism now. Students who do *not* have such previous experience will look to each other and to their professors for help.

This represents a moment of profound opportunity, a moment in which the uncertainties and searching of professors trying to meet the diverse demands of their positions can come together with the questions and vocational needs of students and, together, mine the traditions (of the church, the academy, and the wider culture) for the resources necessary to move forward. Indeed, this is an opportunity to make accessible and make manifest in the ways Boys calls for. But the invitation to make accessible and make manifest is not primarily about scholarly study but about theological leadership in communities of faith (understood broadly to include the kinds of leadership our students will provide in social service agencies, in political contexts, and so on).

Consider our goals as seminary professors. We are preparing pastors who stand in continuity with those who have gone before them and will maintain the churches already begun; we are nourishing leaders for a missionary church in a global context; we are preparing scholars who will sustain critical research into pressing theological issues; and we are educating leaders who will bring theological insight to the wider culture. In order to teach well in such a context, we need to learn how to listen carefully and thoughtfully, profoundly and deeply. We need to reclaim all of the practices of discernment and attentiveness. There is much wisdom in our various traditions upon which to draw, including the traditions of academic research, if only we can listen well.

The concluding project of many schools participating in The Lexington Seminar has been to create time and space in which to listen. During a period in which great emphasis is being placed on strategic action and theological schools are under enormous pressure—from financial concerns, theological conflicts, technology divides, and so on—it might seem counterintuitive to ask for quiet, listening, and reflection, but these are precisely the gifts of theological communities that we are most in need of in the wider culture and thus precisely the resources we most need to cultivate as teachers of and for the church.

Many solutions to today's challenges grow out of learning to listen to the central claims of our traditions and communities and finding ways to bring the skills we have already gained as scholars to the task of teaching and supporting learning with our students. In the following sections, I note briefly discussions of listening in the wider literature and then turn to what we have learned about listening from the many Lexington Seminar projects. Finally, I propose a framework for encouraging deep listening in a range of theological contexts.

Learning from Listening

First, what exactly do I mean by listening in the context of this essay? Following on the work of Vella (1994) and Boys, and adding to them from the wider literature, listening refers most directly to a reflective, dialogical, engaged form of communicative interaction that is an essential element of transformative education. Scott Cormode (2006), who writes of "making spiritual sense," demonstrates such listening in action. Other pertinent scholars who write about reflective practice include Brookfield (1995, 2006), Schön (1990), and Heifetz (1994). It is referred to in the work of the Common Fire project, which speaks of "responsible imagination" (Daloz et al. 1996) and can be traced in the patterns of appreciative inquiry (Branson 2004) and the analyses offered through narrative therapy (Freedman and Combs 1996).

Perhaps more urgently, for the contexts in which theological educators learn, listening—and discerning through listening—can be traced throughout the biblical narrative. Think about the haunting words of Samuel (1 Sam. 3:10): "Speak, for your servant is listening." Think, too, of Mary's patient and faithful response to the astonishing visit of the angel in Luke. But their listening was not simple acquiescence, as can be seen even more vividly in the actions of many of the prophets—my favorite being Jonah, whose first response was to run away. The psalms themselves, particularly the more painful of the lament psalms, are urgent attempts to communicate to a God whom faithful people believe in but often cannot fathom.

Frank Rogers (1997, 114–116), writing of the process of discernment, says:

> The history of the church is littered with the stories of people who have claimed guidance from the Spirit when the prejudices of self-deception reigned instead. From the earliest days of Judaism and Christianity, awareness of this danger has prompted faithful people to articulate criteria by which to judge the authenticity of claims regarding the Spirit....

- fidelity to Scripture and the tradition
- fruit of the Spirit
- inner authority and peace
- communal harmony
- enhancement rather than extinction of life
- integrity in the process of discernment

It is this form of listening, a listening that takes seriously the community in which it seeks an answer, that is so crucial for teaching in theological education. Indeed, this form of listening requires a certain kind of suspension of judgment in order to be open to the presence of persons with whom we are joined in the activities of learning. Kegan and Lahey (2001, 141) describe a series of deconstructive propositions that are illustrative:

- There is probable merit to my perspective.
- My perspective may not be accurate.
- There is some coherence, if not merit, to the other person's perspective.
- There may be more than one legitimate interpretation.
- The other person's view of my viewpoint is important information to my assessing whether I am right or identifying what merit there is to my view.
- Our conflict may be the result of the separate commitments each of us hold, including commitments we are not always aware we hold.
- Both of us have something to learn from the conversation.
- We need to have two-way conversation to learn from each other.
- If contradictions can be a source of our learning, then we can come to engage not only internal contradictions as a source of learning but interpersonal contradictions (i.e., "conflict") as well.
- The goal of our conversation is for each of us to learn more about ourselves and the other as meaning makers.[1]

This form of listening—discerning, nonjudgmental, open to learning—meets some very specific challenges that researchers have identified in the teaching/learning process. Cognitive neuroscientists, for instance, have described the ways in which learning something requires building upon previous experiences, previously laid-down neurological pathways (Zull 2002). In order to determine what elements of material to share and how best to share them, teachers must first understand where students are in relation to a particular subject and then carefully shape educational interventions that can build on what they know—or critique it if necessary—en route to new learning.

Such assessment must begin from a receptive place rather than from a need to establish immediate authority. As Kegan (1994) notes, the process must first confirm a student's meaning—in other words, teachers must first demonstrate that they can enter into the student's world and understand it on its own terms—before seeking to contradict the meaning that student is making. Ultimately, of course, even the contradictions must flow into a newly organized continuity, or the student's sense of meaning can become rigid and fragile.

Consider just some of the many challenges faculty teaching in theological schools face when addressing student preparation:

- Classrooms containing students who know nothing of the biblical canon alongside students who have memorized huge segments of it.
- Students with no experience of, or respect for, traditional religious expression alongside students for whom any questioning of the tradition elicits deep fear.
- Students with significant spiritual experiences in a limited array of worship contexts alongside students with few such experiences but a much wider set of worship contexts.

In each of these instances, the best approach for one student might be the opposite of that for another student. What is a teacher to do? In many cases, we simply ignore the differences and attempt to present the same content in the same manner for all students, trusting that students (who are, after all, graduate students) will come to a satisfactory interpretation on their own. Unfortunately, such a practice rarely leads to success, and indeed much of the current crisis in communities of faith has to be attributed, at least in part, to leaders who are not adept enough at adaptive responses to adequately engage their congregations. Much learning grows from the so-called implicit and null curricula: we learn from *how* we are taught and by what is *not* taught just as much as through any explicit content. Professors who cannot model for their students how to meet them where they are, respecting and challenging them into new growth, teach their students how to be leaders who are *not* adaptive. Here Cormode's work (2006) is particularly helpful, showing ways into adaptive and hermeneutical leadership formation.

So what might be the alternatives? How can we, as theological educators, listen carefully enough and wisely enough and then work clearly enough in response that we can reach more of our students in ways that are healthy and helpful? One of the key insights of educational literature more generally, particularly as relates to education reform, is that relational trust is a crucial component of successful change (Bryk and Schneider 2002;

Brookfield 1995, 2006; Brookfield and Preskill 1999; Palmer 1983, 1998). The challenge within theological education, then, at least in terms of creating more effective learning environments, is to build and sustain relational trust, and the first step in that process is learning to listen deeply and well.

Encouraging Faculty to Listen Deeply

Schools participating in The Lexington Seminar have built relational trust by listening in multiple ways. They have listened to their past, they have listened to each other, they have listened to their students, they have listened to the churches they serve, and they have listened for the signs of the time.

Listening to One's Past

Many theological schools have difficult conflicts in their history, and faculty tend to shy away from revisiting such conflicts for fear of opening old wounds or getting stuck in recurring quagmires. On the other hand, theological education has experienced enough turnover lately that many newer faculty members know little about the history or deep stories of their institutions. Therefore, several schools participating in The Lexington Seminar chose to revisit their history—while avoiding the risk of opening wounds—by asking questions about *generative stories in learning* from the institutions' pasts.

Thus, Methodist Theological School in Ohio (MTSO), seeking to revise its grading practices, began to wonder more deeply why its curriculum had been shaped as it was and what its institutional identity really meant in relation to the curriculum. In seeking to answer such questions, the faculty delved into the original founding materials of the institution (which was born in 1958), spoke with trustees and students, and spent time in retreats. Many of MTSO's key founders were deeply involved in the field of religious education, and their original commitments to demonstrable learning outcomes gave the MTSO's faculty a new way to think about evaluating students. The faculty's conversation about assessment broadened and deepened and was enriched by listening to the stories of why and how the institution had been founded. By so listening the faculty retrieved and reclaimed an understanding of learning that drew them into a more extensive and ongoing evaluation of their own work, as well as that of students. As MTSO's final report notes (2003):

> One important thing to happen through this project is that by talking about the ways we assess students, teachers were also engaging in assessment of their own practices. By gathering data on our individual and institutional GPAs, we began to move beyond anecdote and suspicion to genuine information. Sharing criteria

for grading in the context of talking about our institutional values has allowed us to assess whether we are in fact doing in our courses what needs to be done in order to achieve our institutional goals. One's classroom is no longer one's own private domain. By making public certain information, it is easier to see how we are engaged in a common enterprise, how each can individually make a contribution to that enterprise, and how self-correction may happen when necessary.

The faculty has now put in place a process of evaluating students that accumulates paragraphs of feedback which are annually reviewed by a faculty advisor and which, in turn, provide both early warning of problems and early evidence of gifts. In this way students entering a degree program at MTSO are provided with more transparency about what is expected, along with more opportunities to correct their course along the way, should that prove necessary.

MTSO has found that its faculty can bring the skills they had learned in academic research to the task of inquiry and listening to their students and larger constituencies and in so doing bridge some of the challenges the face:

> It is likely that many other theological schools feel the same tension that we do between accountability to the church and to the academy. While our work on identity questions is not yet complete, we are learning some ways that this tension can be productive. Mooring in the academy requires us to evaluate students according to its accepted standards, and mooring in the church reminds us that within the educational world we have a specific role to play. Theological schools mark a unique intersection between religious life and the larger culture, and this peculiar situation allows for conversation and integration that is increasingly important for a pluralistic world. Fruitful conversation and integration cannot take place if our two constituencies are played off against each other or if one is relegated to a place of diminished importance. In order for theological schools to fulfill our potential, we need to embrace the dual identity that we have. (Methodist Theological School in Ohio 2003)

Gordon-Conwell Theological Seminary is another example of a school deliberately seeking insight from its past into dilemmas in its present. Struggling to figure out a way to better approach integration and spiritual formation issues, the faculty undertook the very intentional process of a spiritual heritage retreat, which invited them into the history of their institution and gave them room to tie that history to the current story that faculty and students are writing together, as they learn collaboratively about spiritual formation and learning. This process not only gave faculty a clearer understanding of the roots of the current institution, but it gave them a plethora of stories to share with their students, inviting them to feel a part of the movement that founded Gordon-Conwell.

This retreat spanned two days and one night and included a New England excursion of evangelical history. Guided by church historian Garth Rosell, sites were visited throughout Northeast Massachusetts and the Connecticut River Valley that are part of the history of such notable figures in American religious history as Whitefield, Edwards, Bradstreet and Moody. Through these discussions, faculty were given occasions to connect their individual and shared stories through four intentional components of the retreat. First, during the rides between sites on the chartered coaches, certain faculty members were assigned ten-minute spots to share their personal journeys of faith. Many of these "testimonials" opened the lives of faculty members to their colleagues in ways that typically do not occur in the seminary routine. Comments in retrospect were that these were some of the more serendipitous moments of the retreat. Second, mini-lectures were given by the faculty on evangelical history in New England at most of the historical landmarks....Third, a former faculty member, Robert Dvorak, was invited to join the retreat and lead several Hymn Sings. In this capacity, he connected the faculty to the revivalistic and evangelical shared tradition as well as demonstrating the importance of such hymnody to American religious history. Finally, each meal was a time for lectures and presentations to be suspended and for faculty to interact with each other and their spouses....(Gordon-Conwell Theological Seminary 2002)

Both MTSO and Gordon-Conwell stepped back and engaged the past by asking questions intentionally aimed at eliciting *generative* stories, which in turn led to creative space opening up in which faculty could try out practices that were new to them but deeply resonant within the institution. Listening led to reclaiming which led to openness to creating anew.

Listening to Each Other

The idea of listening to each other might seem too obvious to note. Clearly, a community of learning needs to learn *with* each other, and that requires deep listening. But the press of daily tasks can often become so difficult that faculties forget to listen to one another.

The narrative written by the Church Divinity School of the Pacific (CDSP) vividly illustrates the overwhelming pressure seminary faculty face dealing with multiple tasks on a daily basis. Further, as CDSP's final report notes, "We realized that a factor contributing to our situation in a fundamental way was that we tend to *assume* a great deal about every aspect of our lives as teachers and administrators, and that the unspokenness of our assumptions elevates everyone's level of anxiety" (2001). One clear solution to such assumptions is to create spaces and time in which rather than assuming shared knowledge, faculty actually build together a culture in which expectations are clear and competing commitments are acknowledged—and that is precisely what CDSP did. After a series of faculty retreats, the school's report notes, "As we mulled over the case we had presented, where a *professor* was being pulled in a number of directions, we began to observe that in many ways, the lives of our *students* looked similar. A consensus emerged that our new curriculum needed to emphasize integration—a focus that would necessitate explicit cooperation between the teachers of the various courses" (2001).

Indeed, in order to teach effectively in environments with diverse students and multiple, often competing, commitments, faculties must learn the art of collaboration. Yet collaboration is hardly a strategy emphasized in doctoral studies, although it is increasingly present in professional research. The strategy that CDSP chose to implement was neither obvious nor simple, but in deliberately choosing to spend time building a culture together, the faculty gained renewed energy and creative passion for their central task of teaching. This is not a solution drawn from mere sensitivity exercises but rather from the rigorous engagement of trained scholars focusing on building together a collaborative culture of learning.

In a similar vein, United Theological Seminary of the Twin Cities joined The Lexington Seminar with the clear intention of focusing on the challenge of helping students integrate their learning, which the school perceived as an integral element of formation. In the process, the United faculty discovered that they needed to make their own assumptions about integration and formation clearer, which meant spending whatever time was necessary working through conflicting ideas about integration. Eventually the faculty chose to institute a series of noontime luncheons in which individual members shared stories of their personal faith journeys in a context in which students and faculty were both present. These lunches came to be a key turning point for the school, creating a climate of energy and interest around the diverse ways in which people walk in faith. It also gave students a plethora of options to consider for their own journeying.

In each of these cases, the pressing need to find a solution to a specific challenge was set aside in favor of creating space for deeper listening to each other. And in each of these cases, that decision led to a climate of trust and respect, which in turn led to more effective solutions, once the original presenting problem was engaged.

Listening to Students

I noted early in this paper that listening to one's students is a key commitment but one that is not often reinforced by traditional academic socialization. Much scholarship on how to attend to student learning is emerging from within more general education contexts. Several schools participating in The Lexington Seminar chose to use such scholarship to shape their projects.

Palmer Theological Seminary (formerly Eastern Baptist Theological Seminary) has been working hard to build a learning-centered curriculum. In part that effort arose from faculty and administrators listening to their students, trustees, and church constituencies and discovering that few of them understood what the curriculum was trying to accomplish and how it fit together. Rather than assuming that its students and other constituencies were deficient in some way or that their teachers were not effective, Palmer decided that the whole curriculum, the whole process of learning, required more transparency. All of the constituencies involved in theological education need to understand what is expected of them and how a specific curriculum will help them achieve their goals.

Thus the faculty developed a clear description of the learning competencies they want their students to achieve based on what they heard from the communities their students will serve and then used that description as a focus for the rest of their curriculum development. Ultimately, they also used that description as an essential element for evaluating students. The many documents they created in the process (including several kinds of writing rubrics, a course template, a course grid, and so on) are wonderful examples of transparency in practice and will likely be useful resources for many other schools.

The process of getting to this place, however, has not been easy. As their final report notes:

> For each of us, the cost of changing long-ingrained habits of teaching and learning is different. Differences between us must be both visible and accepted if we are to move into new habits of teaching and learning. We need to know what we're dealing with not simply in our students, but with each other....
>
> As a faculty, the cost of radical changes in the way we teach and learn isn't worth it if our goal is to find a quick fix to the way we do our educational business, or to make a big splash in the small pond of Western theological education. We must do this work from our hearts, or not engage it at all. It takes time, energy, willingness to live with ambiguity, and some uncertainty about how we will accomplish our long-range goals. (Eastern Baptist Theological Seminary 2000)

The process of listening to students, to outside constituents, to each other—and the resultant action undertaken in response—is neither easy nor without pain. But deep listening also makes clear that resources are present that a community may draw upon in its work together.

Bethel Theological Seminary also chose to make major changes in its curriculum after listening to students with a keen ear for their development. The seminary was in the middle of a major restructuring during its participation in The Lexington Seminar. Among other processes, it was creating a Center for Spiritual and Personal Formation. Students in Bethel's programs are now required to participate in courses through that center, and an intentional process is in place for assessing how students are progressing through the curriculum goals in formation. One element of that process involves the faculty—at every faculty meeting—being invited to attend to how students are learning. Where a challenge or deeper dilemma emerges for a specific student, a process is now in place for creating a developmental plan that a student can follow to address the identified challenge. Presenting the process in a positive light has been a key element in its success. Students see it not as punitive but as a step forward in their continuing learning. As Bethel's final report (2001) notes:

> Systemically, the faculty response to this vision seems to have energized students as well. Students seem to be more convinced of the importance of formation and integration and therefore more willing to open themselves to the process. They have volunteered more stories, with more gratitude for their experience, than ever before.

In each of these instances, the process of listening was deliberately shaped not to invite shame or criticism but to elicit genuine curiosity about what and how students were learning and in what ways faculty might shape and strengthen their learning. What was heard was then acted upon with creative and generative effort.

Listening to Churches and Congregations

It is clear that teaching during times of intense change also requires listening in contexts larger than one's immediate context. As other essays in this book are focusing on institutional issues (see, in particular, Dr. Bessler's essay), I will not spend much time on such listening. Still, it is worth noting briefly that two schools have made specific efforts to move their faculty outside of their walls in attempts to help them reconsider how their teaching ought to be focused. In the case of Palmer Seminary, systematic outreach to the school's many constituencies was the fuel that ignited a shift to learning-centered pedagogies. The Harvard Divinity School has also chosen to use its Lexington Seminar grant to take its faculty members out to visit several of their students' field education sites. The project has just begun, but interim reports suggest that the faculty at Harvard are finding the visits powerful invitations to genuine curiosity about the contexts in which their students will serve and to new innovations in the ways in which they teach specific content.

Listening to the Signs of the Times

Perhaps the most difficult listening is that of listening to the signs of the times. It is difficult precisely because the pace of change today is so rapid, the elements of such change so multiple, and the immensity of the task so overwhelming. Most scholars manage their inquiries by focusing on a limited area of study and carefully specifying its parameters. Such limits and parameters evolve over time amid the careful demands of academic disciplines. The signs of the times, on the other hand, have no easy limits and few appropriate parameters. Yet precisely because the *evangelion* continues to breathe among and through us, the challenge persists. Many of the schools participating in The Lexington Seminar have tried various ways of listening to their context.

Most of them, even ranging far afield, come back to their central resources—their students and the communities from which their students come and to which they will be sent. Listening carefully to students not only makes teaching more effective, it encourages faculty to look with fresh eyes at the ways in which faith is being practiced, the gospel is being heard, and the *missio dei* is emerging among us. Ultimately, such listening can only strengthen our vocation as theological educators.

Deepening Vocation to Support Learning

When I began this essay, I noted the sharp mismatch between the ways in which seminary professors have been prepared through doctoral study and the preparation that today's students bring to the classroom. Many of my colleagues bemoan such preparation, believing it to be less than helpful and, in some instances, actually harmful to theological study. It is certainly true that few of today's students come with deep and lifelong immersion in vibrant communities of faith, and even fewer come with extensive backgrounds in philosophy and ancient language study. They do, however, come with vivid relational abilities, active engagement in much of media culture, and a passionate faith in Jesus Christ. That they have such faith suggests that they have had experiences from which we can learn and which they ought to be prepared to share. It also suggests that opportunities might exist for faculty to walk alongside students and invite them into the questions we study, the resources we have to share. Indeed, there are opportunities in students' passion to give them access to the tradition and make manifest for them the ways in which the tradition is ever transforming, including the very ways in which the students themselves will transform it.

This concern over preparation and necessary skills in turn leads back to the essay's larger question: how do we help professors develop beyond their academic training into teachers who are appropriately present in seminary settings? The answer is to come to a new understanding of what it means to profess—indeed, to come to a new recognition of what it means to confess—faith in the context of graduate theological education.

Far too many of us prepared for our current vocation by studying in university contexts in which confessing our faith was not central to academic study, and we have also learned from previous destructive history—in which confessing faith was not an invitation to learning and transformation but rather a premature closure of such exploration and study—that confessing faith and conducting academic research do not easily mix. We are quite understandably reluctant to cross these boundaries and step outside of what remains scholarly discourse in the guilds. Yet the primary reason that many of us are teaching in the seminary context is that we *do* have a faith we confess, and our academic studies have nurtured that faith in ways we want to share. Faith is a powerful resource—and should be used as such—as we struggle with the teaching challenges we face. We need to learn to traverse the boundaries between faith and academic rigor with our eyes open and our hearts afire, without letting go of the critical lenses we have acquired along the way.

Faculty in seminaries are struggling to help our students prepare to become leaders in a world sorely in need of Christ's saving grace and the justice that emerges from it. As such we must unlearn much of what we were socialized into in the midst of academic contexts and open ourselves up to the transformation that grows out of learning *with* our students. Rather than avoiding conflict or managing it through rigid dances in tightly structured guild contexts, we must learn how to navigate through the difficult currents of ordinary, everyday conflict and find ways to nourish our own vocations as scholars and teachers in the midst of such conflict.

Here the skills we have learned as scholars are very useful, if we can approach our own embodied, emotional selves with a friendly degree of distance and reflection. Stephen Brookfield is particularly noted for his ability to communicate within his work the very tangled emotions that arise while teaching and, further, to suggest constructive ways in which to use them as additional insight. Parker Palmer has also worked this ground, his writing on the inner landscape of a teacher being especially pertinent. In both of these cases, talented master teachers lead their readers through the daily, ordinary tensions of the classroom and find in such tensions generative insight for effective teaching.

Brookfield's use of the critical incident inquiry demonstrates, unfortunately, how often we misunderstand our students and how such misunderstanding can lead to problematic learning (Brookfield and Preskill 1999). That insight, in turn, leads to a clearer recognition of how important it is to *listen well* to our students, and ultimately, to the communities from which they come and to which they are being called.

Still, even this listening is not enough. As theological educators, we must attend yet another form of listening, and it is that form—nourished by biblical narratives, supported by life in community, broken open and shared in table fellowship—that finally brings us to the still point in this process. So much of academic guild practice ignores or even trivializes the life of the Spirit that it can be easy to think that teaching in a seminary is simply another academic practice, albeit in a context in which one uses religious vocabulary. Seminaries are *not* research universities, although they share some characteristics with them. It is precisely this element of shared seminary life—the life of the Spirit lived in community—that is most often ignored within academic research and guild settings.

Nourishing and sustaining our vocation as teachers in seminaries has to begin in a clear recognition of this distinctive element of seminary life. Putting this recognition front and center in our shared endeavor can vivify and challenge all of our teaching practices and lead more thoroughly to learning-centered work.

Appreciative Inquiry: A Model of Listening for Teaching in the Life of the Spirit

The key shift this essay proposes to help schools implement is a cultural one. We need to help seminaries build places for reflective conversation, places that support engagement with learning practices that grow organically throughout a learning institution. An essential element of such conversation is respectful listening, in a variety of places and with a variety of conversation partners. Such conversation takes time—which is often a rare and valuable resource in contemporary seminaries—and so it must be built into the daily fabric of the place, not as a special or episodic kind of inquiry.

An important element of the cultural shift being sought here is to create a deeper vocational connection between faculty members' academic training and the part of their current role that requires them to teach, which demands of them that they support learning with their students. Given that very little of most professors' academic training allows for such a connection, let alone seeks to deepen and expand upon it, this is tricky ground, often prone to inciting all sorts of vulnerabilities. For that reason, most of the schools of The Lexington Seminar have sought to use what social scientists would label an "appreciative inquiry" methodology in their projects. So, too, do the ideas presented here.

Perhaps a brief explanation of this methodology would be helpful by way of introduction. Most academics are familiar with problem-based research methodologies, which, when applied to pressing challenges, seek to identify specific problems, diagnose the conditions or dynamics that lead to such problems, and then strategize appropriate responses. In theological contexts, this process is often envisioned as a circle that includes the steps of naming the current condition or situation, critically reflecting on that situation, putting that situation into relationship with the Christian story, and then visioning renewed engagement with the situation through Christian life, before once again naming a problem. Such a process can be extraordinarily fruitful, and has given birth to myriad differing theological insights. The process described in this essay, however, comes at a particular situation from a different angle.

First, rather than beginning by naming a problem—a process that in many cases can lead to ever more painful recognition and "stuck-ness" *in* the problem for a time, rather than engagement with the ground beneath, around, and above it—appreciative inquiry seeks to initiate, inquire, and imagine into the generative dynamics already present in a situation. Examples of the kinds of inquiry that are sought in appreciative methodologies include the following:

- What made the situation *generative* for you?
- What is the *best* example you can think of?
- If a complaint is coming to mind, what would be the *positive* goal not yet achieved.

Tim Tennent has quoted in this volume Craig Dykstra's series of questions to seminaries (1999). The first among them is, "What is God doing in the world?" This is followed by, "What does the church need to be like in order to align itself with what God is doing in the world?" Appreciative inquiry is congruent with such questions, because the first step in any such process is *inquiring* into those dynamics of a given situation that lead to gratitude, that shape the organization's hope and thankfulness.

There is pressing need within theological schools to ask what God is up to in ways that delight in the answers and that seek to make the process of listening both central and tenable. Mark Lau Branson has written at length about such processes in church settings. His work is foundational in theological contexts, and his book-length treatment of the topic—*Memories, Hopes, and Conversations: Appreciative Inquiry and Congregational Change*—is an appropriate place for a leadership team to begin. Branson argues, for instance,

> The church in Thessalonica was under two kinds of external threats: religious persecution and social pressure.... Paul's pastoral admonitions indicate that these environmental forces were dangerous because they tempted the church to capitulate to fear...and seduction.... But Paul's letter does not begin with the problems and his pastoral solutions. Rather, he begins with thanksgiving (1 Thess. 1:2–10; 2 Thess. 1:3–4; 2:13).... Paul wants his readers to begin with this frame of gratefulness, this opening prayer of thanksgiving, so that his pastoral

initiatives can be properly understood. The life-giving resources that they need are not just external, they are available in their own practices, and through their own narratives. (2004, 44–45)

By contextualizing the process of inquiry within the biblical narratives that shape a seminary's life—indeed, in the very process of offering thanksgiving to God—the process is situated at the heart of what seminaries are engaged in.

Second, the goal of the process is in many ways the process itself. That is to say, the journey is the reward. Appreciative inquiry is most effective in situations in which the very warp and weft of a culture needs to shift, and where the processes used to make such a shift are intended themselves to become a constituent part of what is sought. Done well, the methodology builds positive conversational buzz of a sort that further highlights and reinforces whatever is discovered within the process itself. Indeed, as Branson notes,

> the thesis of Appreciative Inquiry is that an organization, such as a church, can be re-created by its conversations. And if that new creation is to feature the most life-giving forces and forms possible, then the conversations must be shaped by appreciative questions. A church's leaders make decisions about what to talk about, what questions to ask, what metaphors to use—and every such initiative shapes the present and the future. (2004, xiii)

Branson writes within theological contexts, about religious organizations, but a similar insight is at the heart of the work of Robert Kegan, whose books—*How the Way We Talk Can Change the Way We Work* (2001, with Lahey) and *Change Leadership: A Practical Guide to Transforming Our Schools* (2006, with Wagner and Lahey)—have had such a transformative impact within educational institutions more generally and whose ideas about "deconstructive propositions" I quoted earlier.[2]

Given the purpose of this essay and the intent to create room for faculty to practice listening in deep and reflective ways, appreciative inquiry provides a set of basic assumptions and practical steps for shaping such listening in ways that can contribute constructively to a seminary's future.

Overview of the Model

The basic model proposed here has six major parts to it and embeds appreciative inquiry within a sequenced outline based largely on the work of Grant Wiggins and Jay McTighe (2005), who write about "understanding by design." (See Figure 3.1.) First, a general process of appreciative inquiry regarding the connections between teaching and the specific metaphors

Figure 3.1: The Appreciative Inquiry Model.

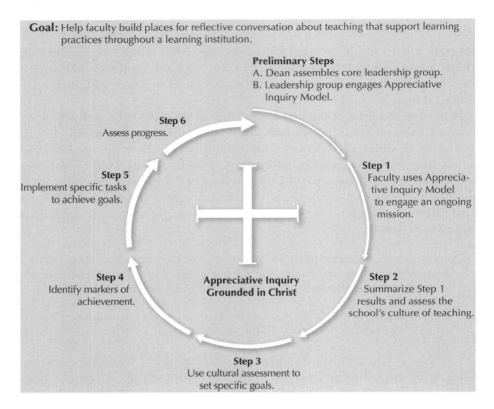

Goal: Help faculty build places for reflective conversation about teaching that support learning practices throughout a learning institution.

Preliminary Steps
A. Dean assembles core leadership group.
B. Leadership group engages Appreciative Inquiry Model.

Step 6
Assess progress.

Step 5
Implement specific tasks to achieve goals.

Step 1
Faculty uses Appreciative Inquiry Model to engage an ongoing mission.

Step 4
Identify markers of achievement.

Appreciative Inquiry Grounded in Christ

Step 2
Summarize Step 1 results and assess the school's culture of teaching.

Step 3
Use cultural assessment to set specific goals.

found in the mission of the school is undertaken. Second, data from that process are studied to assess the current culture around teaching in the school. Third, an overall goal for this instance of the cultural intervention is chosen. Fourth, adequate demonstrations of such a goal—markers of achievement—are identified. Fifth, specific learning tasks are undertaken to achieve the overall goal. Finally, assessment of the overall effect is identified. Following that, the cycle can be repeated.

Preliminary Steps: Or, Begin at the Beginning!

To begin, the person in the school who is most closely tasked with supporting faculty development around teaching should work with the president and board of directors to ensure that they recognize that stimulating the kind of cultural change proposed here takes time and must be understood to be an ongoing process of formation. In most schools this person is the academic dean. Even if the academic dean decides to delegate most of the work of this model to a trusted partner, the dean must take the lead in ensuring that the president and board understand and support the long-term process, for there is no quicker way to kill the process than to demand that it bear fruit immediately. Expected outcomes and long-term goals need to be identified in ways that are manageable and flexible, allowing for ongoing evaluation of progress without setting up unrealistic expectations. Reading the Branson book (2004) might prove to be a fruitful shared task at this juncture.

The next step is to identify—again, in collaboration with the leadership of the school—one key meaning-making process currently taking place. Perhaps the school is working on revising its mission statement or perhaps it is time for a curriculum review. Every ten years or so a school must do a self-study for the ATS; perhaps that process is ongoing. Or perhaps the school has had a major change of leadership and is currently getting to know its new leader. Whatever the case, the dean needs to identify a process that contains the following key elements:

- It is a process in which the whole school is already engaged.
- It is a process that takes seriously the stated mission of the school.
- It is a process that looks toward the future.
- It is a process that is not explicitly tasked with improving teaching.

The meaning-making process must be something that lies at the heart of the school's mission but not something that is so narrowly focused as to be only about teaching.

After identifying the process, the dean and others should strategize ways to implement an appreciative inquiry component into the process that will elicit stories about teaching. For most schools, such strategizing is likely to occur in one small group session within a larger faculty retreat weekend or perhaps a series of small group sessions that form part of a larger strategic planning mode, but the groups should include all members of the faculty. For example, a faculty of forty can be divided into five groups of eight. (More specific examples of such strategies can be found in the school narratives and reports available at http://www.lexingtonseminar.org/archive/index.php on The Lexington Seminar's Web site.)

To lead the small group discussions, the dean should recruit one faculty colleague to help facilitate conversation in each group. In recruiting facilitators, the dean should look for people who meet the following criteria:

- They enjoy talking about teaching in positive ways.
- They have small group facilitation skills.
- They are not notably embedded in any divisive current debates at the school and are thus perceived by colleagues to be open and fair.
- They come from a range of positions and ranks, such as pre-tenured, tenured, and administrative.

The first goal of these facilitators, who in many instances will form the dean's leadership group for the model, should be to familiarize themselves with the appreciative inquiry (AI) process and practice using it together to reflect on their own teaching practices and vocation within theological education, thus building their own skills and cohesion as a group. If the budget allows, the school should ask this group to meet regularly and pay for snacks at the meetings as well as reading resources or other tools. (Reading the Branson book together would be a good initial assignment for this group too).

Begin the Whole-Faculty Process

Once the small leadership group is comfortable with the AI process (which will likely take at least a term if not an entire academic year), the group will be ready to undertake the larger task with the whole faculty, taking each step one at a time.

Step One: Appreciative Inquiry Linked to Mission

Using the appreciative inquiry script (see Appendix at the end of this essay), the leadership group will invite the faculty to participate in the AI process in tandem with whatever larger, ongoing process has been previously identified. (If, for example, the school is in the midst of a self-study, the leadership group can use the AI process to generate stories of teaching as one element in that process.) If the academic dean is *not* leading a small group process, it should nonetheless be clear that the dean and the school administration generally are authorizing and supporting this intervention.

The primary goal of this first step is to create a favorable buzz regarding this kind of inquiry. Faculty should enjoy the process of learning something from each other in ways that are neither competitive nor fraught with fear. The first step should also reinforce the central theme or concept (such as self-study, strategic planning, or curriculum review) that is being explored but do so through a discussion of teaching. Luther Seminary, for example, chose to use the two terms "mission" and "confession" in their AI process as a way of contributing to strategic planning. They used the AI process to explore some of the ways in which "mission" and "confession" were generative within teaching and then folded that information back into strategic planning.

Using the AI process to explore a central metaphor from the school's mission lays the groundwork for more direct engagement with faculty vocation on teaching, but in this initial stage the focus on teaching is secondary to the primary work being engaged by the faculty. There are, however, several outcomes being sought in this process that are specific to improving teaching:

- Giving faculty practice in talking appreciatively about teaching in a nonthreatening environment.
- Generating data for a basic assessment of the culture surrounding teaching in the school, particularly the way in which "talk about teaching" occurs in the school.
- Generating data about the connection (or lack thereof) between the primary mission of the school and faculty perceptions of their vocation as teachers.

Step Two: Cultural Assessment

After the conclusion of the larger effort (such as a faculty retreat) in which the AI process has occurred, two important tasks must be completed. First, a general summary of what was learned needs to be returned to the faculty, preferably in a setting in which it can be further discussed; second, the leadership group needs to plan their next steps. There are multiple examples within Lexington Seminar project schools of ways to communicate what has been learned in this initial kind of process, such as voluntary brown-bag luncheons and faculty workshop discussions. The key is to find a context that is invitational rather than mandatory. At this point in the process, it is helpful to have the summary communicated by the dean, thereby demonstrating that that person is listening well to what faculty are saying. It is also helpful to create a resource list in some place accessible to faculty, describing the various constructive practices that were identified during the AI process and helping faculty to connect with each other to learn from them. In this way faculty can see a visible, helpful outcome before the entire process is even well under way.

The second task, which grows directly out of the summary, requires the leadership group to develop for itself a clear sense of what was learned about the culture of teaching in the school. Using what was learned in the AI process as well as what is known already about structures at the school, what can the leadership group say about the current culture of reflection (or lack thereof) on teaching at the school? The leadership group should use the following questions to help assess the school's cultural context:

- What kinds of "talk about teaching" currently take place in your institution?
- What is the "tone" of the talk? Negative? Fearful? Gossipy? Constructive? Helpful?
- Where does the talk occur? How is it begun?
- Who seems genuinely engaged by the process of supporting student learning?

- Who has formal responsibility for faculty development around teaching? To what extent is that person involved in informal conversation about teaching?
- Whom do new teachers go to for help as they begin their teaching?
- To what extent are senior faculty able and willing to talk about their own teaching practices?
- What seem to be repeating themes in generative stories about teaching?

Step Three: Setting Specific Goals

The next step is to draw on the cultural assessment to create specific goals for the school. Figure 3.2 (Reflective Practice Matrix) can be especially useful in helping determine how the school behaves within the matrix and how the group would like to see the school change. Keep in mind that it is rare, if not impossible, for behavior to jump from the extreme left of the matrix to the extreme right without demonstrating some or all of the intervening behaviors. The goal, therefore, should be to progress one step at a time. It is also crucial to use this chart as an invitation for growth, not as a tool for shaming. It might be appropriate to use this rubric only within the small leadership group, or if it is shared with the larger faculty group, then it should be accompanied by appropriate preparation and with an emphasis on recognizing what the faculty has already achieved, rather than how much more it can grow. The leadership group should endeavor to keep the focus appreciative.

Some possible goals to consider include the following:

- Moving away from complaint to thoughtful sharing
- Building informal spaces for constructive talk about teaching
- Moving from constructive to deconstructive criticism
- Building structures for ongoing reflection
- Inviting students, staff, and congregations into the process of reflecting on teaching

At this point in the process, it is *not yet* time to plan concrete events. The focus should remain on choosing a specific goal to be achieved, given the current context. To be realistic, it is best to focus on one or two areas in which to work on growth. The overarching goal is to shift one category to the right in at least one row of the matrix.

Step Four: Identify Markers of Achievement

Once a discrete, well-defined goal has been identified, it is time for a second round of inquiry to establish clear markers that would demonstrate whether the goal is being achieved. The following are examples of suitable markers:

- A generally positive buzz about teaching
- Faculty who can collaborate together across the curriculum
- Faculty who regularly attend meetings on teaching enhancement
- Students who rave about their learning experiences
- Faculty who participate in professional conferences on teaching
- Faculty who write about teaching as part of their scholarly research
- Faculty peer-group course enhancement teams

Here again invitational brown-bag luncheons, options during faculty retreats, and so on are very appropriate formats for such an inquiry. At this time the task is to name concrete ways that the community can demonstrate that the goal is being met. This is the point in the process at which the dean and the process's leadership group should check in with the leadership of the school (specifically, the president and the board of directors) to assure that the identified goals are appropriate and that the markers of achievement are clearly agreed to and understood in advance of their being pursued.

Step Five: Implement Specific Tasks

At this point, the dean and the leadership group can begin to implement specific learning events that will help the faculty move toward the desired goal. The Lexington Seminar archives (http://www.lexingtonseminar.org/archive/index.php), as well as the books published out of The Lexington Seminar and the Keystone Conference (Klimoski 2005; Warford 2004), are full of narratives and other reports that can offer ideas for how to do this.

Here the task becomes one of identifying learning processes—events, workshops, moments in the daily life of the community—that will help faculty develop the necessary ideas, motivation, and skills to achieve the stated goal. One example might be moving from a process of evaluation of teaching that is only a postmortem once a class has concluded to deliberately inviting evaluation along the way. What would it take to help the faculty do this? At Luther Seminary, for instance, a small group of colleagues who were already familiar with each other and interested in talking about teaching began to meet regularly over lunch to talk about evaluation during a class as well as at the end of it. They eventually shared ideas about using critical incident (CI) inquiry reports, one-minute papers, and so on, leading to a much larger experimentation with ongoing evaluation throughout the faculty. The creation and sustenance of this small peer-group learning-enhancement team was the specific strategy put in place to achieve the larger goal.

Figure 3.2: Reflective Matrix: Spectrum of Reflective Practice in Seminary Teaching.

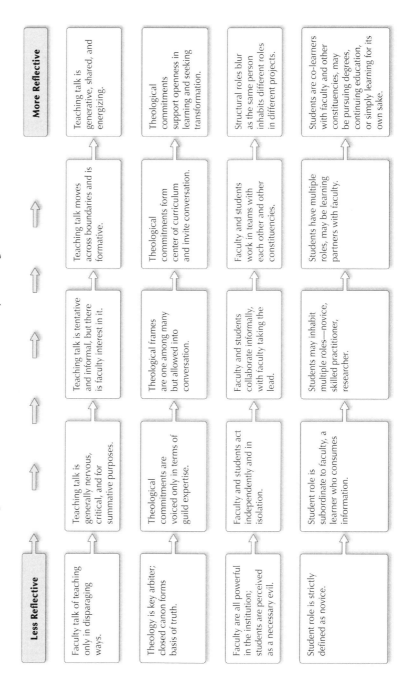

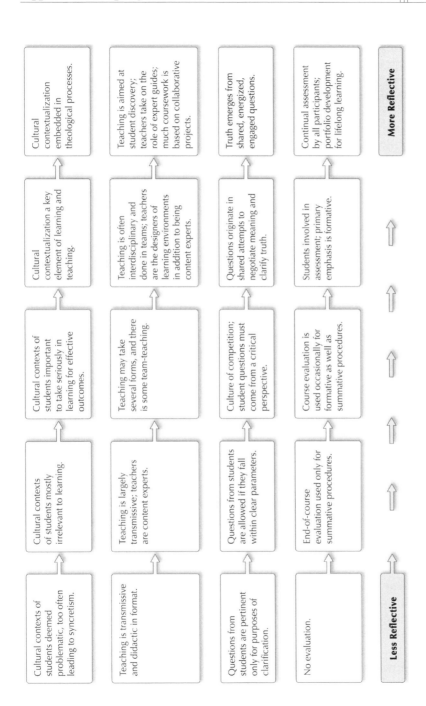

Examples of other specific tasks include the following:

- Create small incentives for peer collaboration on teaching.
- Institute a teaching-learning brown-bag luncheon series.
- Provide a structured opportunity during a faculty retreat to talk about teaching.
- Extend the reach of conversation about teaching and learning to include students and congregations.
- Provide regular information about outside opportunities for enhancing teaching.
- Sponsor small grants for research into classroom practices.
- Take the opportunities that present themselves to highlight good teaching practices.

Step Six: Assessment

It is difficult to specify a timeline on this kind of cultural intervention, because each process will be situated in the unique context of a specific school. Whatever the timeline, however, it is important to have moments identified for evaluating the manner in which the process is unfolding and determining the extent to which specific steps might need to be modified. Assessment at this point grows pressing, because the leadership group will need to begin thinking about the next round of inquiry and goal development.

At a minimum, the academic dean ought to invite another conversation with the president and the relevant board members, before repeating the cycle of inquiry and planning. The next time the cycle begins, the appreciative inquiry process need not be situated within another process, for the school may have moved along enough to explicitly engage a process of reflection on teaching.

To reflect on the entire process just completed, keep in mind the following important points:

- The faculty cannot move from the far left side of the Reflective Practice Matrix to the far right side without moving through intervening steps. The process is developmental and must be taken from one step to the next.
- The method is appreciative inquiry, so it is crucial to support faculty in this process, which can be one of much vulnerability.
- Emphasize the positive elements of reflective practice. Do not deny the negative but turn the complaint into a statement of commitment to something positive. For example, turn "I hate it when small groups are just students sharing ignorance" into "I yearn for small group discussions in which students engage deeply with the texts in front of them."

- Work from the underlying, shared commitment and use language (such as theological language) that is appropriate to the context.
- Kegan's work is very useful here, because it highlights a way of engaging the language (1994, 2001). Parker Palmer's trust circles offer one useful model (1998, 2005) Brookfield's critical incident inquiry reports offer yet another (1995, 1999, 2006).

Conclusion

The goal of this model is to invite faculty into sustained—and sustaining—reflection upon their vocation as teachers within the context of theological education. The appreciative inquiry guidelines provide a process for doing so, and the larger model outline provides a structure and sequence, but the primary goal is one of listening. As I noted at the beginning of this essay, that listening must eventually be shaped by attending to the history of the institution, to the seminary's students, to the churches and congregations that send students and to which students are called, and to the "signs of the times." Giving faculty experience with the practice of listening—first with each other—invites them ever more deeply into the practice, and from there it is virtually inevitable, as the narratives and reports of The Lexington Seminar schools document, for these other kinds of listening to occur.

Appendix

Appreciative Inquiry Process: Script for Small Group Leaders

Introduction

Leadership can take place as we create environments for surfacing our questions and as a community forms responses and stories that are generative of energy and renewed commitment in relation to those questions.

Many concepts and ideas wind their way through our work at [name of school], but one that seems to have been at the center of much of our recent discussion is [name a central metaphor, mission statement, etc.].

Clearly this [concept or metaphor] is not static, or easily defined, and how it is woven into teaching can differ from one person or one context to the next.

In this process we're exploring how we work with the dynamic tension of [concept or metaphor] in the teaching and learning processes at [school]. We're interested in knowing how you work with this dynamic (if you do) and what this concept means for you when it's generating positive energy in your teaching. In other words, while there are times to discuss how things go wrong, this process is about the *best* positive examples and narratives regarding your teaching.

During our small group time we'll ask each group to think from an overview frame first, then move to elicit specific ideas about discrete value. Next, we'll ask you to choose from what you've shared something that you would identify (at least at this moment, in this conversation) as most important. Finally, we'll invite you to generate some wishes or dreams that point toward where [school] could go in preparing to teach in ways that support [concept or metaphor].

Overview

In all the ways that you've experienced the dynamic of [concept or metaphor] at [school], tell me about a *positive* experience that highlights your engagement with the dynamic. What can you say about ways in which [concept or metaphor] has been generative for you here at [school]?

[Note: If the small group does not find this concept creatively dynamic or cannot think of a single positive experience with it, then ask for a positive story about the school more generally. This is an overview question, so the stories do not need to be about teaching but more generally about engaging the concept or metaphor in question.]

What makes that generativity possible? What had to happen to make it work? What was the context? Who was involved?

Value

Next we'll move to ask more specifically about [this concept or metaphor] in the context of teaching at [school].

In your experience, what is the best example of [this concept or metaphor] as it arises in the midst of a teaching process, such as a class, a text you have read with students, or something students have done?

What can you tell me about the example? What made the engagement with [concept or metaphor] work so well? What had to happen to make it work? Who was involved? What about the context made it possible? Why do you think it was generative?

Can you think of some other good examples?

[Note: Ask for additional good examples; seek more detail.]

Most important

Next, think about these elements you've just identified—the pieces that made that story, that example of [concept or metaphor] work so well in a teaching context. Of all the things you've just identified in relation to that story, what would you say is the single most important factor in the generativity of engagement with [concept or metaphor] in your teaching? What do you think made it work?

Would you like to add anything about that single most important element?

Wishes

Keeping your ideas positive, imagine three wishes that, if fulfilled, would help [school] best achieve its mission. [Read the school's mission statement.]

What would your three wishes be?

[Note: The key here is to invite the small group into imaginative engagement with a positive future. If the group goes instead to complaint, make them tell you what the future would look like if the complaint were reversed, that is, if there were a rich abundance of the thing the complaint identifies as lacking. If participants complain even about the desire to stay on the positive in this part of the process, point out that our sacred texts have embedded complaint in gratefulness and that at this moment you are seeking stories of gratefulness, even if, and perhaps especially if, they are clearly dreams or yet-to-be-fulfilled wishes.]

Notes

1. A similar set of principles can be found in the "Principles of Dialogue" from the Catholic Common Ground Initiative (http://www.nplc.org/commonground/dialogue.htm) and in the ELCA's document "Talking Together as Christians about Tough Social Issues" (brief excerpt available online at http://www.elca.org/youth/resource/riskydiscussions.html).
2. There is an abundant and rich literature on the use of appreciative inquiry. Mark Lau Branson's book, noted earlier, is an excellent introduction. Within the broader literature on organizational development, see also Bushe (1995) and Ludema (2001).

References

Bethel Theological Seminary. 2001. Project Narrative. http://www.lexingtonseminar.org/archive/archive_doc.php/doctype/report/id/271/

Boys, Mary. 1989. *Educating in Faith*. San Francisco: Harper & Row Publishers.

Branson, Mark Lau. 2004. *Memories, Hopes, and Conversations: Appreciative Inquiry and Congregational Change*. Herndon, VA: Alban Institute.

Brookfield, Stephen. 1995. *Becoming a Critically Reflective Teacher*. San Francisco: Jossey-Bass.

———. 2006. *The Skillful Teacher: On Technique, Trust, and Responsiveness in the Classroom*. 2nd ed. San Francisco: Jossey-Bass.

———, and Stephen Preskill. 1999. *Discussion as a Way of Teaching: Tools and Techniques for Democratic Classrooms*. San Francisco: Jossey-Bass.

Bryk, A., and B. Schneider. 2002. *Trust in Schools: A Core Resource for Improvement*. New York: Russell Sage Foundation.

Bushe, Gervase. 1995. "Advances in Appreciative Inquiry as an Organizational Development Intervention." *Organization Development Journal* 3 (3): 14–22.

Church Divinity School of the Pacific. 2001. Project Report. http://www.lexingtonseminar.org/archive/archive_doc.php/doctype/report/id/272/

Cormode, Scott. 2006. *Making Spiritual Sense: Christian Leaders as Spiritual Interpreters*. Nashville: Abingdon Press.

Daloz, Laurent A. Parks, Cheryl H. Keen, James P. Keen, and Sharon Daloz Parks. 1996. *Common Fire: Leading Lives of Commitment in a Complex World*. Boston: Beacon Press.

Dykstra, Craig. 1999. *Growing in the Life of Faith: Education and Christian Practices*. Louisville, KY: Geneva Press.

Eastern Baptist Theological Seminary (now Palmer Theological Seminary). 2000. Project Report. http://www.lexingtonseminar.org/archive/archive_doc.php/doctype/report/id/268/

Freedman, Jill, and Gene Combs. 1996. *Narrative Therapy: The Social Construction of Preferred Realities*. New York: W. W. Norton & Company.

Gordon-Conwell Theological Seminary. 2002. Project Report. http://www.lexington-seminar.org/archive/archive_doc.php/doctype/report/id/277/

Heifetz, Ronald. 1994. *Leadership without Easy Answers*. Cambridge, MA: Belknap Press of Harvard University Press.

Kegan, Robert. 1994. *In over Our Heads: The Mental Demands of Modern Life*. Cambridge, MA: Harvard University Press.

———, and Lisa Laskow Lahey. 2001. *How the Way We Talk Can Change the Way We Work*. San Francisco: Jossey-Bass.

———, Tony Wagner, and Lisa Laskow Lahey. 2006. *Change Leadership: A Practical Guide to Transforming Our Schools*. San Francisco: Jossey-Bass.

Klimoski, V., K. O'Neil, and K. Schuth. 2005. *Educating Leaders for Ministry: Issues and Responses*. Collegeville, MN: Liturgical Press.

Ludema, James. 2001. "From Deficit Discourse to Vocabularies of Hope: The Power of Appreciation." In *Appreciative Inquiry: An Emerging Direction for Organization Development*, ed. D. L. Cooperrider, P. R. Sorensen, T.F. Yaeger, and D. Whitney. Champaign, IL: Stipes Publishing L.L.C. Also available online at http://www.stipes.com/aichap29.htm.

Methodist Theological School in Ohio. 2003. Project Report. http://www.lexingtonseminar.org/archive/archive_doc.php/doctype/report/id/292/

Palmer, Parker J. 1983. *To Know as We Are Known: A Spirituality of Education*. San Francisco: Harper & Row.

———. 1998. *Courage to Teach: Exploring the Inner Landscape of a Teacher's Life*. San Francisco: Jossey-Bass.

———. 2005. *A Hidden Wholeness: Welcoming the Soul and Weaving Community in a Wounded World*. San Francisco: Jossey-Bass.

Rogers, Frank M. 1997. "Discernment." In *Practicing Our Faith: A Way of Life for a Searching People*, ed. Dorothy Bass. San Francisco: Jossey-Bass.

Schön, Donald A. 1990. *Educating the Reflective Practitioner*. San Francisco: Jossey-Bass.

Vella, Jane. 1994. *Learning to Listen, Learning to Teach: The Power of Dialogue in Educating Adults*. San Francisco: Jossey-Bass.

Warford, Malcolm L., ed. 2004. *Practical Wisdom: On Theological Teaching and Learning.* New York: Peter Lang Publishing.

Wiggins, Grant, and Jay McTighe. 2005. *Understanding by Design.* Alexandria, VA: Association for Supervision and Curriculum Development.

Zull, James, 2002. *The Art of Changing the Brain: Enriching Teaching by Exploring the Biology of Learning.* Sterling, VA: Stylus Publishing.

4. The Ministries for Which We Teach: A World Café Model

Timothy C. Tennent

Maps of the world produced by Europeans during the medieval period are strikingly adorned with beautiful Christian images, and they situate Europe and the Mediterranean at the center of the map. Much of Africa and Asia, however, is not even represented, and the few distorted land masses that vaguely represent the southern continents tend to blend hazily into the margins amid drawings of savages, dog-headed kings, and grotesque demons. These maps reveal as much about the medieval Western worldview as about its cartography. Undoubtedly, our cartography has improved dramatically over the years, but it seems that our "ecclesiastical cartography" has not kept pace (Bonk 2004). Theological institutions are often myopic when it comes to seeing with clarity the world to which we have been called to minister. Most people are naturally resistant to change, and, despite the growing emphasis on globalization and overall sensitivity to diversity in theological education, numerous ecclesiastical blind spots still need to be addressed.

The focus of this chapter is to explore the growing disjuncture between the apparent purpose of teaching and learning in the various settings we call "seminary" or "divinity school" and the actual ministries to which our students are called. In order to be theological teachers who equip the ministries of the church, seminary faculties must discover a broader and deeper gospel that can be relevant to the missionary character of local ministries while also proclaiming and nurturing faith throughout the world. In particular, this means considering how our pedagogy is shaped by and expresses essential theological and missional aims. Martin Dowson and Dennis McInerney (2005, 403) contend that the current models of ministry are not preparing students for the new ministries that are needed. Samuel Escobar (2004, 143) echoes this concern when he raises the question, "Are seminaries educating students for Christian ministry in the world as it *is* or the world as it once was?" In the past, questions concerning the relation-ship of teaching and learning to ministry contexts were primarily framed as pedagogical questions in the narrow sense of instructional technique. The particular value of Escobar's essay is that he points out that in the twen-ty-first century such pedagogical issues are in-depth questions of theology and mission, which are the fundamental matters for which we teach. In this regard, to engage pedagogy is to address the teleological questions of purpose and meaning. This chapter explores these observations, seeking to understand how the settings, methods, content, and goals of theologi-cal education must change in light of the changing array of ministries for which we are preparing students to serve.

The World Is in *My Parish*

It is not uncommon to hear complaints about the lack of connectivity between ministerial preparation and the actual ministry settings our stu-dents are entering. For example, David Tracy laments what he calls the "three great separations of modern Western culture," all of which have served to separate the task of theological education from actual ministry contexts. According to Tracy, these three "fatal" separations are the "sep-aration of feeling and thought, the separation of form and content, and the separation of theory and practice" (1998, 235). However, postmod-ernism and globalization have created complex new forms of connectivity in which to reflect on the training for and context of ministry. Christian ministry has never occurred in a vacuum, but the forces of globalization have created a situation in which every local context is today informed by the larger global context. Globalization has been summarized as a com-plex connectivity whereby local events and social relationships are influ-enced and shaped by distant events (Tomlinson 1999, 2). This complex connectivity has influenced every sphere of life, including politics, social relationships, economics, technology, science, culture, and religion. Today, even if you are the pastor of a small church in Kansas, you still cannot think about your ministry apart from the larger global context. Indeed, part of the power of globalization is our increased awareness of complex connectivity.

We live in a world of iPods, instant messages, YouTube, chat rooms, MySpace, and Facebook. Such a world has produced a new kind of global connectivity that is very different from the metanarratives of modernism, which produced a single grand canopy of meaning. The church and the message of the gospel are often reduced to just another message among thousands that might give meaning to a person's personal narrative. They can no longer pretend to be a normative claim for the world.

Globalization has also brought the world into a new kind of connectivity that our parents' generation could hardly have imagined. Dramatic new forces of migration, especially since 1965, have brought thousands of new peoples into the Western world. Many of these ethnic groups represent the fastest-growing Christian groups in the West. John Wesley said, "The world is my parish." Today we must amend that by saying, "The world is *in* my parish." The challenge for theological education is to learn how to teach for this kind of ministry.

The Post-Christian West and Post-Western Christianity

The two major trends that serve to frame today's ministerial settings can best be summarized by the twin phrases, "post-Christian West" and "post-Western Christianity."

The phrase "post-Christian West" is an acknowledgment that in the last few decades Western civilization has been undergoing an unprecedented transformation, with dramatic implications for theological education and ministerial preparation. The West is experiencing a reaction against the Enlightenment that has produced a growing skepticism about the certainty of knowledge, an increasing distrust in history, and a general cultural malaise caused by the loss of meaning. In 1979, the French philosopher Jean Francois Lyotard coined the term "postmodernism" to describe these changes (1985). According to Lyotard, the twin forces of Christendom and the Enlightenment provided the foundations for the modern world and gave Western societies a cohesive sense of an overarching truth informed either by a theistic, Judeo-Christian worldview or a secular belief in the inevitability of progress, the reliability of human reason, and the perfectibility of humanity. Western Christianity and the Enlightenment, though sometimes in conflict, often supported and drew strength and energy from one another. The key shift from modernism to postmodernism, argues Lyotard, is marked by the collapse of what he calls these "grand narratives," which had guided and produced stability in the formation of modernity. Students who were entering seminary shared many of the assumptions of these grand narratives, and ministerial preparation took place within the stability of this larger context. Today, the rise of pluralism, the effects of postmodernity, the loss of faith in the inevitable progress of the human race, and an increasing uncertainty about normative truth claims have resulted in a crisis of ministerial training. The old plausibility structures are collapsing. We now live in the midst of the denouement of Western Christendom that has served as the dominant paradigm for Christian ministry in the West since the time of Constantine. We must discover (or rediscover) a new kind of faithfulness to the gospel in a post-Christendom, post-Christian West.[1] We are now sending our graduates into a dramatically different context than was present a generation or two ago. To what degree, therefore, should this changed setting and context of ministry influence the methods, structure, content, and goals of theological education today?

The phrase "post-Western Christianity" indicates that we are simultaneously witnessing a stunning rise of Christianity outside the West, coupled by a precipitous decline of Christianity in the West. This change is often referred to as a shift in the center of gravity of the world Christian movement. After its birth in Asia two thousand years ago, Christianity experienced vigorous growth as it moved steadily westward and northward. However, beginning in 1900, the statistical center of gravity began to shift dramatically southward, and in 1970 it began to move eastward for the first time in 1,370 years. Sixty-seven percent of all Christians around the world are now located outside the West, in the Majority World (Johnson and Chung 2004). According to Philip Jenkins, these new Christians generally have a great respect "for the authority of Scripture, especially in matters of morality; a willingness to accept the Bible as an inspired text... [and] a special interest in supernatural elements of scripture, such as miracles, visions and healings" (2006, 4). As Peter Berger has said, "To put it simply, experiments with secularized religion have generally failed; religious movements with beliefs and practices dripping with reactionary supernaturalism have widely succeeded" (1999, 4).[2] The French writer Gilles Kepel (1994) has aptly called this dramatic turnaround the "revenge of God" (*la revanche de Dieu*). As Harvey Cox has noted (1995, 103), "If God really did die, as Nietzche's madman proclaimed, then why have so many billions of people not gotten the word?" A global Christian revolution is occurring outside the Western world, and most Western Christians are only gradually beginning to realize the full implications of this shift.

It is likely that the twin themes of post-Christian West and post-Western Christianity will continue to mark the first half of the twenty-first century, and possibly even beyond. These twin themes are best dramatized by the growth of the church in Africa and the decline of the church in Western Europe and North America. From 1970 to 1985, for example, the church in Africa grew by more than 6 million people. During that same time, more than 23 million people left the church in Europe and North America, equaling a rate of 4,300 people per day (Sanneh 2003, 15).[3] Similarly, while India and China currently have approximately 60 million and 90 million Christians, respectively, it is estimated that both countries will have over 150 million Christians each by 2050.[4] The following graph (Figure 4.1) shows the dramatic rise of Christians from the global South.

Despite this reality, we still tend to view *our* Western theological training institutions as the center of the ecclesiastical universe. We continue to

Figure 4.1: Changing Percentage of Christians in North and South: AD 33 to AD 2100.

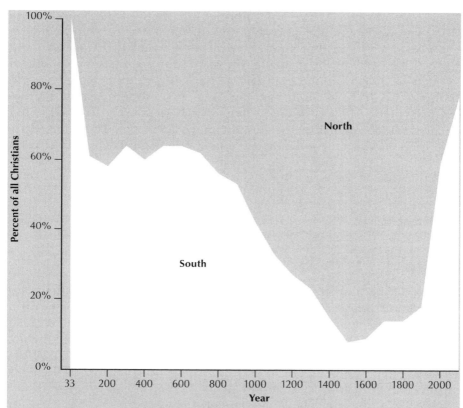

Note: North is defined here in a geopolitical sense by five current United Nations regions: Eastern Europe (including Russia), Northern Europe, Southern Europe, Western Europe and Northern America. South is defined as the remaining sixteen current UN regions: Eastern Africa, Middle Africa, Northern Africa, Southern Africa, Western Africa, Eastern Asia, South-central Asia, Southeastern Asia, Western Asia, Caribbean, Central America, South America, Australia/New Zealand, Melanesia, Micronesia, and Polynesia.

Source: Johnson and Chung (2004).

vastly overestimate the role of our trained pastors and theologians in the actual work and calling of Christian ministry. We continue to talk about our church history and our schools in a way that puts North America and Europe at the center, and whatever is happening outside the West is reserved for those preparing for the mission field or church historians who want to pursue specialist studies. We continue to think that our theological reflections are normative and universally applicable to all people. In short, the Western church has been slow to understand how the dramatic shifts in the demographics of global Christianity are influencing what constitutes normative Christianity.

The slowness of the Western church to recognize these new realities should not be taken as a pessimistic assessment of the church in the West. The West continues to have a vital role in education and theological enquiry, which has a profound effect on the global Christian movement. Indeed, it is precisely because the role of Western seminaries is so influential that we must continue to reflect on our complex and changing world. In fact, it would be an overstatement to say that Western seminaries have not been aware of many of these changes or have not felt the need to find creative ways to address these new realities. For example, the theme for the 1986 biennial meeting of the Association of Theological Schools (ATS) was "Global Challenges and Perspectives in Theological Education," and the keynote address was given by Cardinal Francis Arinze from Kenya. David Schuller sums up the complex challenges facing ATS seminaries:

> At the beginning, we naively thought that the adoption of a few courses on world religions; the enlargement of bibliographies to include more theologians from South America, Africa, and Asia; greater sensitivity to women; and a few more sabbaticals in the Third World countries would solve the problem. (1993, 1)

However, it became clear that the sheer complexity of the challenges of globalization, pluralism, postmodernity, and the shifting center of gravity of the world Christian movement required a more thorough reexamination of the prevailing assumptions about theological education. We still inhabit a kind of theological fantasyland that obscures an honest assessment of ourselves and the new global realities. Addressing this collective ecclesiastical myopia is a difficult process, and we need ongoing encouragement to view our life and work from a larger, more global perspective.

Teaching and Learning with a Global Consciousness

None of the narratives developed for The Lexington Seminar during 1999–2006 focus explicitly on the growing globalization of the world Christian movement. Nevertheless, several of the narratives tacitly acknowledge the challenge. For example, Trinity Evangelical Divinity School (2003), founded in the Swedish Free Church tradition, now has 28 percent international students who, as Trinity's narrative points out, do not understand why the Swedish festival of Santa Lucia is so important in the life of the Seminary. Virginia Theological Seminary's narrative (1999a) openly reflects on how difficult the transition to seminary life in the West was in the experience of an international student from Kenya. Finally, a Harvard Divinity School professor is taken aback when a Haitian Pentecostal student asserts that his mother "was possessed by one hundred and twenty-one spirits" until she was "liberated" by Christianity (Harvard Divinity School 2006). The global church is now arriving at our seminaries, and, increasingly, it is insisting that its voices be heard.[5]

Gordon-Conwell Theological Seminary, where I teach, resulted from the merger of two institutions—Gordon Divinity School and Conwell School of Theology. Gordon Divinity School was founded as a missionary training institute by A. J. Gordon in 1889. Conwell School of Theology was founded in Philadelphia in 1884 by the Reverend Russell Conwell, a prominent Baptist minister who was well known for his famous sermon and book, *Acres of Diamonds*, which focused on the need to find "acres of diamonds" in your own backyard. Conwell's vision was to encourage Christians to live out the gospel right where they were, which, in his case, meant being faithful in the midst of urban Philadelphia. A. J. Gordon's vision was to train and send missionaries to bring the gospel to the ends of the earth. The merger of Gordon and Conwell was, in effect, the joining of the backyard with the ends of the earth. This is the challenge for all theological institutions today. We must simultaneously find new, creative ways to send forth ministers to serve our local constituencies but do it with an eye to the rest of the world, because our backyard must touch the ends of the earth.

The challenge of becoming simultaneously more local and more global[6] is an exciting one because never before have seminaries or divinity schools had such a rich diversity of students already present in the classroom. Today's students are remarkably diverse in terms of educational background, ethnic and cultural heritage, and ecclesiastical experiences. This is a well-documented trend evident throughout ATS schools (Klimoski, O'Neil, and Schuth 2005, 1–25).[7] Increasingly, our classrooms are beginning to look far more like the global church, which has important pedagogical implications for the training of ministers.[8] This greater diversity of background, heritage, and experience in the classroom helps to expose areas in which our reflection has been biased and resistant to the actual teachings of scripture. It also becomes an important training ground for preparing ministers for the actual contexts of ministry, because, increasingly, our congregations in the West are also beginning to reflect these new global realities. Western Christianity, especially the mainline, urban churches, are sometimes stereotyped as dwindling congregations in high-steepled churches with graying memberships. However, many of these churches are sharing facilities with thriving Hispanic, Chinese, Korean, or African churches who meet at alternative times or spaces and are contributing to the renewal of Christianity in the West. Philip Jenkins in *The Next Christendom* documents the increasing role immigrant communities are playing in the emergence of a revitalized Western Christianity. In 1930, the United States was the home of 110 million whites, 12 million blacks, and only six hundred thousand categorized as "others" (Jenkins 2002, 100). Only seventy years later, more than 35 million

Americans are now counted as Hispanic and nearly 12 million are Asian. By 2025, Jenkins predicts that 25 percent of the population of United States will be Hispanic or Asian (Jenkins 2002, 100). This shift is having a dramatic influence on the church.

In Cambridge, Massachusetts, close to where I live, the numbers of those who worship Jesus Christ on a typical Sunday morning in a language other than English exceeds those who worship in English. This transformation is happening not only in the traditional immigrant regions of the Northeast and the Southwest but throughout the entire country. The population of Houston currently comprises at least 25 percent who are foreign born—including, for example, eighty thousand Nigerians—compared to only 3 percent foreign born in 1960 (Jenkins 2002, 101, 208). This fact has important implications for seminaries and divinity schools, especially those that are situated in an urban context. Christianity in the West is changing dramatically, and it is a change that has gone largely unnoticed. Nevertheless, there is a growing realization that the emerging new ethnic communities in our midst are playing a crucial role in revitalizing the life of Western Christianity and stimulating more mature theological reflection.

The Incarnation as a Model

The greatest paradigm for this new vision of theological education is, of course, the Incarnation itself. Andrew Walls notes that the incarnation is not just that God became a man but that God became *a particular man* (Walls 1996, 27). There is no generic incarnation. There is only the very specific one in which God in Jesus Christ took on particular flesh and lived in a particular culture and spoke a particular language. Yet Jesus embodied a universal message that embraces every culture, language, and people.

In the same way, seminaries today must pay simultaneous attention to both the universal and the particular. Western theology has at times, in the words of John Mbiti, been "kerygmatically universal, but still theologically provincial" (Mbiti 1976, 6). In other words, we have a central proclamation (kerygma) in the Bible, which is universal, but the theological reflection, systems, and ministerial training that we have drawn from the biblical message have often been overly provincial.

Western theology was, quite appropriately, focused on answering Western questions—often philosophical ones—which were essential for sustaining Christian faith. Unfortunately, because of the long sojourn of the Christian center of gravity in the West, Western theology began to be regarded as universally normative. Eventually, a rather provincial Western theology was propagated around the world as normative and universal. The church outside the West accepted this for many years because of the sheer dominance of Western peoples in the overall global movement. For example, when William Carey, widely regarded as the father of the modern missionary movement, went to India as a missionary in 1793, only 2 percent of the world's Christians lived in Asia, Africa, and Latin America combined. Today, however, with Christianity withering away in the West and the majority of Christians now being located outside the West, a new way of thinking and acting must be embraced. Christianity is on the move, creating a seismic change that is literally changing the face of the whole Christian movement. Every Christian in the world, but especially those in the West, must begin to understand how these changes will influence our understanding of the ministries for which we are training men and women in our seminaries and divinity schools. Once we realize that we are no longer at the center of the world Christian movement, then we can, once again, recapture the missiological nature of our tasks as educators and trainers.

Because the seminaries and divinity schools of the West were for so long situated at the center of the Christian movement, it is easy to see how they came to the false impression that the Western experience and expression of Christianity was somehow normative for all Christians everywhere. It is also clear from the writings of Christians who happened to live in places which, in their day, were at the very center of global Christianity, that they fully expected that Christianity would always be dominant where they lived. The mission field would always be in *other* places and with *other* people. Indeed, during the height of the West's major cultural and geographic expansion, it was probably unimaginable that a day might come when Christianity would wither away in the West. One hundred years ago listeners would have been incredulous to hear someone say that before the end of the twentieth century the historic William Carey Memorial Church in Lester, England, would be a Hindu temple. One hundred years ago it would have seemed highly unlikely that by the dawn of the twenty-first century there would be more evangelicals in Nepal than in Spain (Barrett, Kurian, and Johnson 2001, 527, 687).[9] One hundred years ago few would have believed that on a typical Sunday at the threshold of the twenty-first century only around 1 million Anglicans would attend church in Great Britain, while more than 17 million Anglicans would attend Sunday worship in Nigeria (Knippers 2003; Gledhill, 2003; Bowder, 2004). Many people once believed that the presence of these new Christians was only an unfortunate byproduct of Western, imperialistic colonialism and that with the end of colonial rule, the church would wither and die in these lands (Robert 2000, 53). Others agreed, insisting that the forces of globalization would secularize the world, and religion would become marginal to twenty-first-century life. In fact, precisely the opposite is unfolding. As this essay has pointed out, in the postcolonial period, the church outside the Western world has experienced the most dramatic growth in history. The modern world has not turned into a secular city, and modernization has not led to the predicted collapse of religious faith. Indeed, even the eminent sociologist Peter Berger has noted that "secularization theory is essentially mistaken" because "the assumption that we live in a secularized world is false." Berger goes on to say that the key assumption of secularization theory, which insisted that "modernization necessarily leads to a decline of religion, both in society and in the minds of individuals...turned out to be wrong" (Berger 1999, 2, 3).

All of this inevitably should stimulate our reflection on what it means to be a Christian in the West and how we are to live out our faith within the context of the new realities of global Christianity. Augustine witnessed the barbarian invasions, realized their significance, and produced his classic *City of God*. We must recognize that we are living in a completely new context. It is all too easy to live and breathe the rarefied air of theological reflection and become isolated from the actual challenges and realities of Christian ministry today. Our churches are more like mission outposts than institutions standing at the center of public discourse. Seminaries and divinity schools have always been more successful in training pastors and teachers than in preparing prophets and evangelists. Today we must teach toward the full array of Christian ministries (Eph. 4:11, 12). Furthermore, our students must learn to see themselves as part of a global movement, a movement in which we stand as learners and partners.

Schools participating in The Lexington Seminar reveal that, while much remains to be done, a growing number of seminaries are introducing courses into the curriculum that expose students to the voice of the emerging global church. Some examples of such courses include Candler's "Global Church in God's Mission," Trinity Lutheran's "The Emerging Global Church," Phillip's "Seminar in Global Christianity," Gordon-Conwell's "Advance of the Church in the Non-Western World," and Austin Presbyterian's "Reading the Bible from a Global Perspective." However, the challenge goes far beyond adding a few courses to the existing curriculum. Indeed, many courses on the global church do not appear in the required core curriculum of the M.Div. degree, thus making it clear that the rise of global Christianity, coupled with the dramatically new immigration patterns into the United States, remain peripheral to the M.Div. training programs among participating schools. As David Schuller (1993) has noted, we need more than a few cosmetic changes.

An examination of curriculum changes in ATS schools in general and The Lexington Seminar schools in particular reveals a continuing interest in and commitment to spiritual formation and to strengthening forms of field experience in ministry. Seminaries have invested considerable effort in building into their curriculum various courses that focus on finding ways to connect seminarians to actual ministerial contexts. For example, Harvard Divinity School offers up to two hundred different approved internship sites that allow each student to develop the arts of ministry through supervised internships in specific field education placements. While involved in field education placements, students are required to take a course entitled "Meaning Making: Thinking Theologically about the Practice of Ministry," in which seasoned local ministers lead small groups of students in theological reflection (Harvard Divinity School 2006–2007, 148).

The problem with the current training is that it often focuses on individual formation without a clear idea as to the goal of this formation and how it prepares men and women for specific ministry contexts. The result is an incongruity between training programs and the actual context of ministry that is needed in the global church.

Theological educators must reexamine the way we think about training and the ministry, setting outcomes for our graduates in the light of global realities. Indeed, the problem cannot be reduced to only an examination of the curriculum. As international scholar Tite Tiénou points out, "The faculty *are* our primary curriculum" (2007). The practical model for transformation that this chapter proposes is not focused primarily on curriculum revision but rather on faculty development. Dozens of schools throughout the ATS have devoted innumerable hours to discussing and implementing curriculum revisions in the last few years. In my view, we have placed far too much hope that a changed or revised curriculum will solve our problems and reposition our seminaries to teach more effectively. While curricular change is often needed, the more profound change will always find its locus in those who teach. I would rather see a transformed faculty than a revised curriculum. This outcome obviously means recruiting a more diverse faculty. However, conceptions of diversity must include not only ethnicity and gender but also background and life experience. We need faculty who will teach even the existing curriculum from a different perspective and vista. The life experiences and perspectives of the faculty have an enormous impact on how any curriculum is taught, and the growing diversity of our students dramatically influences what is being learned and the potential ministry settings for which our students are preparing.

A transformed faculty will also learn to be more collaborative as teachers. We teach in disciplines that are highly specialized and that reward individual teaching, achievements, rank, and publications. The DNA of most theological institutions is, therefore, highly resistant to collaboration. We often occupy our own intellectual silos and serve our respective institutions almost like independent contractors. However, a number of theological institutions are exploring more creative and integrated approaches to teaching and learning. For example, a student at Union Theological Seminary in New York will be learning to preach in a homiletics class on the very same passage that he or she is studying in an exegesis class. Similarly, the Methodist Theological School in Ohio (MTSO) has started an initiative whereby faculty share their syllabi with one another. MTSO has also had several faculty conversations on how their coursework can function more collaboratively. Team teaching is also on the rise. Schools as divergent as Harvard Divinity School and Gordon-Conwell are increasingly promoting team-taught classes, using professors from different disciplines. This approach helps us to interact more collaboratively and to understand how members of the same faculty might approach a topic differently because of their own background or perspective. All of these examples remind us that curriculum does not teach students; faculty teach students.

Being Teachers and Learners

One of the most important tasks for theological educators is to remember that we are teachers of the church as well as learners from it. As teachers of the church we have the dual responsibility of faithfully reminding the church of the historic gospel while also helping the church "resist the temptations of cultural, political, and geographical provincialism" (Shriver 1986, 8). As learners, we must always listen to the church. Stephen Neill, the late bishop of the Church of South India (CSI), defined the church as the "community of the redeemed which exists in space and time" (Neill 1952, 205). Christian faith is expressed not only in propositional truths about God's acts that are taught faithfully to the church, but it is also an organic expression of real people who hold a living faith in the resurrected Christ. The need for a more intentional and creative collaboration with the church is essential for a seminary or divinity school to remain healthy and flourish.

This essay opened with the assertion of Dowson and McInerney that the current models of ministry are not preparing students for the new ministries that are needed. This observation reflects a long-standing tension that has always existed between the academy and the church. Tertullian asked, "What has Athens to do with Jerusalem....What has the academy to do with the church?" (Tertullian, *Praescr.* 7.9). Christians have long been aware that the pursuit of academic knowledge about God and the scriptures is not necessarily the same as preparing men and women for effective ministry in the church. This theme appears in many of The Lexington Seminar school narratives. For example, a student in one of the narratives says to the dean, "My call is to serve the church, not the academy" (Lexington Theological Seminary 2002). A student in another narrative says that the seminary is doing a great job "training for further graduate education," but "it is not providing the best possible training for people who will serve as pastors and in related ministerial roles" (Calvin Theological Seminary 1999). Eastern Baptist Theological Seminary (2000) expresses what many schools are experiencing when the dean says in the narrative, "We have students, especially international students, who experience a conflict between piety and scholarship."

Indeed, the disconnect between the seminary and the church is one of the dominant themes underlying many of The Lexington Seminar narratives. This point is expressed most poignantly in the Claremont School of Theology narrative (2000), which recounts the story of one of its students who is invited to preach at his home church during Christmas break. The church had provided a scholarship to help the student through seminary, so the congregation eagerly looks forward to his preaching. The student preaches on a text and, using the "Claremont Way," proceeds to tell the expectant congregation that the text contained teaching that was "dubious," "narrow minded," and "naïve." Later, the church leader calls up the administration at Claremont and angrily asks, "What do you people think you are doing over there at that school?"

However, the rise of a post-Christian West and a post-Western Christianity means that this concern takes on an even greater urgency. In this new context there must be a more collaborative creativity between the seminary/divinity school and the wider global church. Seminaries have traditionally been structured around the assumption that the country is largely evangelized and that there is an existing network of churches prepared to receive our students and employ them for service in specific ministry placements. However, we are now facing a situation in which the global church is younger and needs expertise in church planting and evangelism, and the Western world increasingly needs reevangelization and a whole new generation of evangelists and church planters to respond to the decline of the traditional, mainline churches that have dominated the church landscape for the past two centuries.

Many of the most urgently needed ministries are currently peripheral to many seminaries in North America, which is largely due to the fact that many seminaries do not see their primary mission as serving the church. Several of The Lexington Seminar narratives reflect this point. For example, in response to a proposal that a course in youth ministries be added to the curriculum, one faculty member says, "I worry that we will lose academic excellence in our programs as we are pressed into responding to the endless needs of the church" (Lutheran Theological Seminary at Gettysburg 2003).

Implementing a Globalized Curriculum

Like many schools participating in The Lexington Seminar, Harvard Divinity School has in recent years undergone a major change in its M.Div. curriculum. A primary motivation behind the curricular changes has been the goal of closing the divide between theory and practice by establishing a more integrated curriculum. However, Harvard seems to be focused largely on closing the gap between theological and religious studies and has still not reflected fully on the reality of an authentic, burgeoning, post-Western Christian movement. While it is true that a few courses are offered that might expose a student more adequately to the global church, these remain elective courses, while the core curriculum remains designed primarily to reinforce relativistic pluralism and does not take seriously the growing particularity of Christian movements in the Majority World.

Other Lexington Seminar schools have recognized that technology can create new possibilities for training the global church. Several schools—such as Bethany Theological Seminary, Eastern Mennonite Seminary, Luther Seminary, Gordon-Conwell Theological Seminary, Church Divinity School of the Pacific, Pacific Lutheran Theological Seminary, and Calvin Theological Seminary—offer online courses that can be taken anywhere in the world. However, even when these distance education courses are translated into other languages, such as Chinese, as with the Gordon-Conwell distance education program, there is no guarantee that the content of the courses is always relevant and contextualized for the realities of the global church. A fuller exploration of what new ministries are required and the implication this has for faculty development, curriculum changes, and teaching delivery methods is necessary if we are to effectively serve the church in the twenty-first century.

I have been on the faculty of a theological college in North India for the last twenty years. Having taught hundreds of Indian students during this time, I have become aware that, whereas my U.S. students fully assume that churches exist throughout the United States to provide positions for them in full-time ministry, my North Indian students prepare for ministry knowing from the start that they will have to plant the church that they will subsequently pastor. The exponential growth of global population, especially in the new, emerging Christian centers of Asia and Africa, coupled with the fact that many of these churches are located in the context of poverty and low education, means that the need for trained leaders is growing faster than any traditional seminary model—regardless of where it is located—can address. In short, from a global perspective, the burgeoning need for new forms of ministry and training cannot be served entirely by seminary graduates. We need to look beyond traditional models of professional ministerial training. We must look for new forms of creative collaboration between the seminary and the church in training tens of thousands of new ministers. This must begin by thinking beyond our normal resident degree programs to new kinds of commitments to the delivery of theological education.

For example, Gordon-Conwell has launched an open access Web site known as the Dimensions of the Faith that provides many core theological courses free of charge to anyone. Another organization, known as Biblical

Training (BiblicalTraining.org), has placed an entire array of seminary courses from many of the leading seminary professors in the country on the Web for free access. A few years ago such an idea would have been met with a chorus of protest over intellectual property rights and the need to safeguard our knowledge and research. However, in 1999, the Massachusetts Institute of Technology (MIT) shocked the educational world by announcing that they had reached an agreement with their faculty to put their courses online for complete access to scholars around the world or even self-learners who just want to sit at their computer and learn from some of the world's brightest scholars and thinkers. This initiative, funded in part by the William and Flora Hewlett and the Andrew W. Mellon foundations, is called the MITOpenCourseware project. MIT's rationale was that they could not think of a better way to further their mission which, as their Web site declares, is "to advance knowledge and educate students in science, technology, and other areas of scholarship to best serve the nation and the world" (MIT 2007). Rather than undermining MIT's mission, open access courses have enhanced and furthered it. Currently, MIT has more than 1,550 courses available online. Theological institutions must learn from MIT's example as we think more creatively about effective delivery systems for theological education in the twenty-first century.

This chapter has argued so far that theological teachers who equip the ministries of the church must rediscover a pedagogy that better expresses the new global context and the growing missional needs of today's church. The final part of this chapter explores a specific model for how this goal might be achieved.

A World Café Model for Alumni/ae Narratives and Conversation

Effective teaching cannot be sustained without some feedback and professional growth in learning how the settings and context of ministry are changing. In fact, ATS accreditation standards now require outcome-based assessment that demonstrates the effectiveness of our teaching (consistent with the stated mission or goals of the educational institution) in the contexts of ministries to which we send our students. This is why alumni/ae are so valuable to an institution. Unfortunately, the value of our graduates has often been relegated to phoning them during the annual fund drive or sending them an envelope once a year, hoping for a donation. The alumni/ae office, if it exists at all, is often embedded within the office of development. This tendency has often been deleterious to a healthy relationship between theological institutions and their many graduates. Actually, alumni/ae are, quite apart from any financial gift they may give, one of the most valuable resources a seminary or divinity school has, for several reasons. First, since they are graduates of the school, they know the institution from the inside. They represent the only group who has experienced the curriculum as a whole. In a very real sense, faculty members only see in part, whereas as graduates, for better or for worse, experience the whole curriculum. Second, upon graduation, alumni/ae are moving into the actual settings of ministry for which we as institutions claim we are preparing men and women. After some years of experience in the ministry, alumni/ae are uniquely poised to reflect back on their seminary education in ways that would not be possible when (and if) they were given an exit interview when they were about to graduate and were asked to reflect back on their education. It seems reasonable that a healthy institution should have a keen interest in talking with alumni/ae about a lot more than money.

Heretofore, it has been difficult to find a setting that allows our graduates to help faculty understand these changes because it involves a potentially awkward situation whereby our former students become the teachers and the teachers become the students. Even though we have been called to be teachers of the church as well as learners from the church, seminaries demonstrate a natural reluctance to learn from the church or the laity or even from our own graduates who serve in ordained ministry. Fortunately, this project creatively unlocks this resistance through the use of the narrative approach so effectively modeled by The Lexington Seminar with the faculties of thirty-nine diverse seminaries and divinity schools between 1999 and 2006.

General Contours of the Project

The 253 theological institutions that currently belong to the Association of Theological Schools are remarkably diverse, not only theologically and organizationally, but also in terms of the size and structure of the faculties, which makes the proposal of a model for faculty development challenging. However, the following model can, I believe, fit a wide variety of settings and is flexible enough to be adapted in many creative ways. I encourage you to use this model (or be inspired in some way to create your own) as a pilot project with your faculty during the next academic year.

This project proposal requires the following participants: academic dean, administrative assistant, twelve alumni/ae, and the entire faculty or a select group of faculty, depending on the size of the school.

The academic dean begins the process by meeting with key leaders from the faculty and staff (or the alumni/ae office, if it exists) who have knowledge of the school's graduates. A process is followed that leads to the selection of twelve representative alumni/ae. These twelve should be divided into four groups of three alumni/ae each. Each of the four groups should be assigned a focus theme along with a brief explanatory introduction that will then be used as the catalyst for developing brief narratives. (More is said later about how the participants and the themes might be chosen and how the narratives are developed.) The alumni/ae are asked to reflect on their years of ministry since their graduation from seminary or divinity school. An administrative assistant to the dean can follow up with the graduates and make sure that they understand what they are being asked to do, as well as convey the details of the project.[10]

Following The Lexington Seminar model, the alumni/ae are asked to develop a one- or two-page narrative that encapsulates a problem or challenge which they have faced in ministry. It should be made clear that this is not intended to be a formal, academic kind of presentation but simply the telling of a story. The narrative can be based on actual events, a composite of several events, or a fictional event that effectively demonstrates the challenges of ministry in today's context. It is important, of course, not to use actual names or places even when narrating an event that actually took place. It is also important that the narrative not exceed two pages—written to be read quickly and identifying the main tensions or issues. (Appendix A at the end of this chapter contains guidelines for the alumni/ae to use in preparing the narrative.) Although a total of twelve alumni/ae are chosen for the project, the visits take place in groups of three. A different set of three alumni/ae would participate in each visit, for a total of four visits. At least four conversations are necessary for an effective penetration of the collective faculty ethos. A single visit (or even one visit per semester) can be easily pushed to the margins and not create lasting change, but a series of four or more gatherings[11] sends a message to the faculty that this process is an institutional priority. Multiple gatherings are also necessary in order for the faculty themselves to become stakeholders and to see the long-term benefit of this kind of engagement. Anything less may be received as just another meeting or another added responsibility. It is vital that the dean, or faculty spokesperson who is chosen to articulate the vision for these conversations to the wider faculty, be convinced that this project will bring the faculty to a better place, a more strategic place, a healthier place, a place that continues to resonate with the core values of the institution.

Each alumni/ae visit is followed by a reflective session that develops short-term technical solutions to the challenges raised, as well as long-term strategic and adaptive changes that need to be made over considerable time as an institution adjusts to new realities in North America and around the world. The four alumni/ae visits culminate in a faculty retreat that focuses on the long-term strategic challenges that have been learned and reflected on in light of global realities. The outcome should be a healthier institution, more strategically structured to prepare men and women for effective ministry. See Figure 4.2 for a graphic presentation of the model.

Figure 4.2: The World Café Model of Faculty Development.

Goal: Assist faculty in reconsidering the practices of teaching and learning for the purposes of ministry in post-Western Christianity.

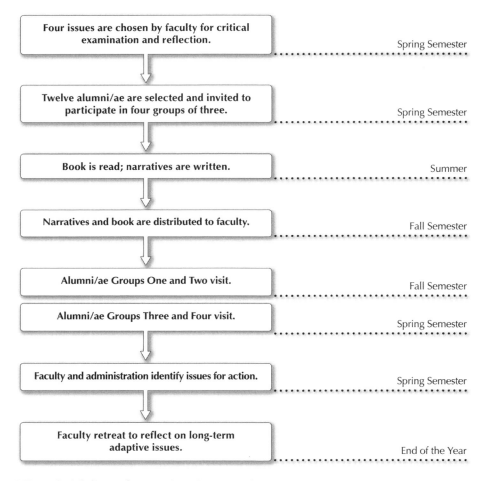

Nine Guidelines for Project Preparation, Execution, and Follow-Up

The following guidelines provide helpful rules of thumb for using this model most effectively.

1. Getting the event into the long-term planning calendar
2. Choosing the alumni/ae participants in the program
3. Focusing and developing the alumni/ae narrative
4. Connecting the narrative to the actual settings of ministry

5. Choosing the right setting for the conversations
6. Preparing for the alumni/ae visit
7. Adopting the World Café Model for the conversations
8. Identifying technical and adaptive problems
9. Structuring the follow-up retreat

Guideline 1: Getting the Event into the Long-Term Planning Calendar

The precise timing of the gatherings will be best determined by the academic calendars within which each particular school operates. However, it is important to work out the exact timing of all the visits in advance and get them on the calendar. Many schools will find the best opportunity to schedule these meetings during mid-September, early November, mid-February, and early April.

Guideline 2: Choosing the Alumni/ae Participants in the Program

The alumni/ae can be chosen through the various formal and informal channels that all schools use to identify graduates. One of the easiest and most cost-effective ways of selecting a representative sampling of alumni/ae is through the snowball sampling method, whereby a few potential alumni/ae are contacted and then asked for the names of others who might be well suited for this kind of interaction. Snowball sampling relies on referrals from an initial group to generate additional alumni/ae.

Regardless of the precise method adopted for contacting alumni/ae, deans should be careful not to limit the names that will be generated only to favorite sons and daughters—that is, graduates who are headed for doctoral work so that they too can become professors and members of faculties. Some of the most remarkable graduates may not have kept in close touch with the faculty after graduation. Consider the following suggestions when selecting participants.

1. Choose participants who have an understanding of the changing contexts and challenges of ministry, such as those alumni/ae who have persevered faithfully in particularly challenging contexts, not merely those who have had easily recognizable successes in ministry.
2. Choose participants from the full life span of ministry. For example, each group of three might include one alumnus/a who has been out of seminary for one or two years, one who has been out for over five years, and a third who has been out of seminary for twenty years or more. Alumni/ae from various stages in their ministry ought to provide richly textured insights into a common theme.

3. Choose alumni/ae from a variety of ministry settings in order to reflect more fully the range of "ministries for which we teach."

Once the participants are selected, the reason for their selection should be articulated to the faculty in order to foster the optimum openness for faculty and alumni/ae to sit down together as fellow learners.

Although it would be ideal to include in the project some alumni/ae serving in the Majority World, financial considerations may prohibit the school from physically bringing back such alumni/ae to participate in the conversations. However, with some creativity and even modest technological infrastructure, it may be possible—through Skype or similar free services[12]—for alumni/ae who are serving abroad to participate fully as members of the alumni/ae groups. Later on, in the culminating retreat, some further ideas are explored for ways to reflect more substantively about the larger global context of ministry today.

Guideline 3: Focusing and Developing the Alumni/ae Narrative

Each of the invited alumni/ae who visit campus will come with a narrative based on a theme that represents a problem or tension which they have encountered in ministry and which the faculty are invited to examine with them and propose solutions collaboratively. Discussions of the narratives may reveal potential deficiencies in the processes of teaching or learning or both. It is important that the narratives are focused within specific areas so that the overall effect after the end of all four meetings at the end of the academic year is to have an overarching strategy for growth among the faculty. The selection of appropriate participants, therefore, is essential to success. Another important component is to give each trio of alumni/ae a theme and a few brief descriptive sentences as a starting point to stimulate their own reflection and to keep the conversations more focused. The academic dean may encourage the entire faculty to generate possible themes about which they would most like to have a sustained conversation. Alternatively, the dean may want to recommend themes more explicitly within the contours of the ATS accreditation standards of assessment. However, the advantage of including the full faculty at this stage is to make them stakeholders and thus encourage greater receptivity for the project. Below are four examples of themes and accompanying notes to the alumni/ae that might be adopted.

Sample Theme 1

Pastoral Ministry in the post-Christian West

Dear [Names of Alumni/ae]:
Thank you for being willing to participate in this valuable project. Please provide a narrative that illustrates how pastoral ministry is influenced,

enhanced, or challenged by the larger context of a post-Christian West. Your narratives should not automatically assume that living as a Christian in a post-Christian West is necessarily a "good" or a "bad" thing. You may want to illustrate in your narrative some painful aspect of trying to be faithful to Christ in this new context. Alternatively, you may want to celebrate some of the new opportunities which we now have in this post-Christendom context to bear witness to Christ.[13] Each of you should prepare a one- or two-page narrative that highlights how your pastoral ministry is being challenged or energized by life in a post-Christian West. I have enclosed a guideline for preparing the narrative.

[Include the narrative guidelines found in Appendix A.]

It will probably be helpful in most settings to send the alumni/ae a complimentary book to help stimulate their reflection on the theme in question and help ground their narratives in good research. In this case, the letter to the alumni/ae could also ask them to read a book related to the theme and then reflect on it in light of their ministry and in developing the narrative. A classic work like Søren Kierkegaard's *Attack upon Christendom* (1968) may be used, or perhaps a contemporary release, such as Peter J. Leithart's *Solomon among the Postmoderns* (2008).

This entire project must be given a solid biblical or theological orientation, which is precisely why academic deans often find that whenever terms like "assessment," "evaluation," or "teaching and learning workshop" are mentioned, they fall on deaf ears. The principal problem is that theological faculties are rarely comfortable with the language, categories, and discourse of the social sciences. Put bluntly, this world is alien to most of the theological guild, which is why, as an integral part of the preparation for the alumni/ae visit, the entire faculty should be given a book to read that provides serious biblical or theological reflection about the chosen theme. The book chosen should relate to the theme that the alumni/ae will be reflecting on, but also expand on it in some significant ways. It may be necessary to consult with faculty colleagues in order to choose the best book for each of the themes. Promoting theological reflection along with the narrative approach will help to further stimulate thoughtfulness along a common theme and yet keep the discussions grounded in real-world, real-life contexts.

Sample Theme 2

The World Is in My Parish: Global Perspectives on the Contemporary Church

Dear [*Alumni/ae Names*]:
Thank you for being willing to participate in this valuable project. Please provide a narrative that illustrates how the changing demographics of

North America is influencing your ministry. John Wesley said, "The *world* is my parish." Today, with the dramatic changes in immigration patterns, we can say, "The world is *in* my parish." We now live in an increasingly diverse society. The celebration of ethnic particularity has turned the melting-pot metaphor of a bygone era into the "salad bowl" or "ethnic stew" metaphor of today. How has this influenced your ministry context? How have these developments challenged or transformed you? What are the implications of this for theological education and ministerial preparation? Prepare a narrative that will help to focus on this issue.[14] I have enclosed a guideline for preparing the narrative.
[*Include the narrative guidelines found in Appendix A.*]

This theme will be particularly helpful to those schools operating in an urban context of dramatic ethnic diversity and change or in churches undergoing shifts in ethnic diversity. Many of The Lexington Seminar narratives focus on the challenges and opportunities seminaries are facing in responding to growing diversity. Here is an opportunity to have a more focused conversation on the same challenge facing society as a whole.

Sample Theme 3

Caregivers and Counselors: How We Are Changing

Dear [*Alumni/ae Names*]:
Thank you for being willing to participate in this valuable project. As pastors, counselors, and caregivers, you regularly come in contact with people who are facing enormous challenges. What, if any, emerging themes are becoming evident? How are families changing, and how should this influence the formation of ministers and theological preparation? How might the gospel provide renewed hope for this generation? Please provide a narrative that illustrates some aspect of these changes that are becoming evident through your personal counseling and caregiving.[15] I have enclosed a guideline for preparing the narrative.
[*Include the narrative guidelines found in Appendix A.*]

This theme will provide an opportunity to include alumni/ae who may not be in pastoral ministry, but who are involved in caregiving. It should be clear that, as with all the narratives, strict confidentiality be maintained in the development of the narrative. The narrative should help to shed light on the broader work of theological and ministerial preparation.

Sample Theme 4

The Life of the Mind and the Cry of the Heart

Dear [*Alumni/ae Names*]:

Thank you for being willing to participate in this valuable project. The pastor as scholar is a paradigm which has long been cherished by seminaries and divinity schools throughout history. Yet, increasingly, the cries for authentic community, for a more holistic approach to life and spirituality, and, above all, for a deepening spiritual experience have caused some to question whether something is missing in current models of theological preparation. Certainly one of the perennial tensions in ministerial preparation has consistently been the role of the seminary in educating the mind as well as forming the heart. Academic excellence and spiritual formation—scholarship and piety—is a tension with which we are well acquainted. Now that you have been out in ministry, how do you see the role of—the seminary in preparing you for ministry? How do you understandfrom your time out of seminary and in the actual ministry setting—the place of the seminary in spiritual formation and personal devotion? Reflecting on your experience and, perhaps, the experience of your colleagues, prepare a narrative that illustrates this tension in some way. I have enclosed a guideline for each of you to use in preparing your narrative.

[*Include the narrative guidelines found in Appendix A.*]

This theme helps to create a context for discussing the growing disconnect between the seminary/divinity school and the church. It may help theological faculties to reflect more transparently about what it means to be a member of a seminary or divinity school faculty rather than a religious studies program of a major university. It may also help faculties better understand why research shows that sixteen- to twenty-nine-year-olds have an increasingly negative perception of Christianity (Kinnaman and Lyons, 2007). Most theological faculties are reluctant to appreciate the fact that even a post-Christian West does not translate into a "secular city." Spirituality and the yearning for authentic religious experience is alive and well in the West. What can we learn about this, and what are the implications for theological education?

The four samples above model the way in which appropriate guidance can be given in the preparation of the narratives.[16] This will help to focus the conversations and make them more than gripe sessions or freewheeling dream sessions not rooted in the practical realities and challenges of institutional life.

The writing of the narratives by the alumni/ae will require some adaptability to fit the variability that exists in the alumni/ae pool. If the three alumni/ae who have been given the common theme live within close proximity to one another, they might meet together and discuss possibilities for a common narrative. However, given the broad dispersion of alumni/ae, it is more likely that each of the participants will write his or her own narrative, which will then be sent to the dean's office and collated with the others. Along with the theme, deans should not forget to send alumni/ae the brief guidelines (see Appendix A) on how to write a narrative. The result will be three separate narratives, all guided by a single central theme. At the end of the entire project there will be a total of twelve narratives, guided by four separate themes.

Once the narratives are submitted, the dean, along with a few representative faculty, should read through the narratives and make any necessary suggestions to the alumni/ae in needed changes or ways the narrative could be improved for a group discussion. Once the narrative is accepted and in its final form, it should be sent, as noted above, to the entire faculty, along with photographs and biographical data for each of the three alumni/ae who will be visiting. The participants should also be given copies of each others' narratives prior to the campus visit.

Guideline 4: Connecting the Narrative to the Actual Settings of Ministry

In interacting with the alumni/ae who are participating in this project and preparing their narratives, it is important to find creative ways for the faculty to be able to visualize the actual ministerial settings where their ministry takes place, thus enhancing faculty understanding of the alumni/ae and enriching conversation at the café gatherings. Suggestions for visualizations are discussed below:

- *Five- to eight-minute video tour.* Most alumni/ae are quite conversant with various video capabilities. They could easily take a few candid clips of the church or the ministry setting or the surrounding streets or neighborhood, which will give the faculty an excellent contextual backdrop for the ensuing conversation. With a TV and VCR or DVD player set up in the room where the conversations will take place, this will easily bring this ministry setting to life. Videos should not run more than five to eight minutes.
- *Five or six PowerPoint slides.* Using a digital camera, the alumni/ae could easily capture a few candid shots of their ministry in the same way as described above. A computer and LCD projector can be prepositioned in the room. As with the video, the presentation should run no longer than five to eight minutes. The importance of such time management should be clearly communicated to the alumni/ae before the visit.

- *On-site hosting of the alumni/ae.* If one of the alumni/ae chosen is within a reasonable distance, then it would be ideal for the conversations to take place right in the setting in which one of the narratives occurs.

Guideline 5: Choosing the Right Setting for the Conversations

The physical setting of these guided conversations will vary based on the particularities of the faculty, but it should be a setting that is conducive to interaction, collaboration, and open discussion.[17] It probably seems intuitive to dedicate a significant portion of an already scheduled faculty meeting for these discussions. Unfortunately, the settings that most faculty use for their regular meetings are often associated with confrontation, boredom, weariness, and bureaucracy. Therefore, a setting should be arranged in a more relaxed, hospitable atmosphere—perhaps, if possible, outside the institution completely. For example, if one of the alumni/ae chosen for the conversation pastors a church nearby, it might be an ideal setting for these conversations.

Guideline 6: Preparing for the Alumni/ae Visit

Prior to the alumni/ae visit, the narratives should be distributed to the entire faculty (another helpful insight gained from The Lexington Seminar projects). Even when, in the case of large theological faculties, only a select group of the faculty were involved in the project, the entire faculty was kept abreast of the project and all were encouraged to participate in the follow-up projects. The inclusion of as many faculty as possible will also help create stakeholders for transformation and change.

Not only should the entire faculty read the narratives and participate in the later conversations, it may be helpful in some settings for the faculty to reflect on the narratives and the key issues involved prior to the visit by the participating alumni/ae. This reflection by the faculty will be more effective if the faculty meet face-to-face to discuss it, rather than exchanging e-mails. When the alumni/ae are then brought onto campus for the guided discussions concerning the issue, the school should pay for their travel and accommodation as well as providing a modest honorarium. A school with even a very tiny budget can always afford to bring in alumni/ae who are within an easy drive. I recommend that the school *not* place the participants in area hotels or on-campus housing, but rather arrange for them to stay in the homes of faculty who have the gift of hospitality. This approach will not only save money, but it will significantly increase the contact time between faculty and alumni/ae. This is a healthy practice, and it will also help to demystify the faculty-student relationship that was created when the alumni/ae were studying at the institution.

As part of a long-term strategy, the dean should notify all of the alumni/ae that this project is taking place, because one of the project's potential benefits is that the project itself can become a story that can be told about the institution. An article featuring the project in the alumni/ae magazine or newsletter will help to deepen the ownership of all alumni/ae in the project, particularly if it can be shown that the project has represented alumni/ae from the full range of ministry settings for which the seminary is teaching.

Guideline 7: Adopting the World Café Model for the Conversations

Once the narratives have been written, the dates are secure for the campus visits, and the locations have been chosen, it is important for the dean, in consultation with others, to adopt a strategy that fosters an atmosphere of collaborative dialogue that can help to discover new ways of thinking and new approaches to problem solving. Juanita Brown and David Isaacs, in *The World Café: Shaping Our Futures through Conversations That Matter* (2005), set forth a model of collaborative discourse that is known as the World Café Model. This model has been successful in a variety of settings and flows out of a commitment to seven principles, well worth reviewing here.

1. The setting must support interaction and engagement.
2. The space must be seen as hospitable.
3. Questions must be significant enough to stimulate collaborative interaction.
4. Everyone's contribution is needed and expected.
5. Cross-pollination of ideas and exploration of diverse perspectives is encouraged while at the same time retaining focus on the core questions.
6. Participants are helped to listen together for patterns, insights, and deeper questions.
7. That which is discovered in the conversations is harvested and shared, and practical steps are explored where specific action can be taken. (Brown and Isaacs 2005, 42–153)

The World Café Model is a flexible, proven, and effective model for fostering collaborative discussions, sharing thoughts, and discovering new opportunities for action and change. It is a resource well worth consulting in preparation for the visit.

Several of these seven principles are integral to the early planning process while others must be made an integral part of how the faculty understands the project and prepares for it. Still others are important in the actual event and subsequent follow-up. The overall effect of this approach will be to help curb the tendency we all have as faculty members to work as independent contractors and avoid the necessary collaborative discussions that are essential to collective change and growth.

When the participants are all gathered together for the event, the conversation should be guided by a faculty member. This person could be the provost or dean, but it may be more strategic to choose another faculty person to guide the discussion. This approach will help to communicate that this is not a typical faculty meeting or a thoroughly top-down initiative. Furthermore, administrators, by virtue of their positions and the tough decisions (such as budget cuts) that they have to make regularly, are sometimes seen as polarizing figures and can inhibit the larger goals of the project. The person chosen must have good people skills and not be socially awkward or defensive in posture. The person needs to have an irenic disposition, be a good listener, and without a reputation of being overly domineering in meetings. Great care should be given *not* to refer to this gathering as a "meeting." Rather, it should be referred to as a "conversation," "learning café," or some other inclusive term. Similarly, the faculty chosen to guide the conversation should be referred to as a "facilitator," not "the chair."

The faculty facilitator should be prepared to provide a warm welcome and a clear, concise (no more than seven minutes) articulation of the purpose of the event. The alumni/ae should each be given three minutes to introduce themselves and state briefly the context in which they serve. (Recall that the entire faculty has already received biographical data on each of the three participants.) Faculty members should be given an opportunity to state their name and their position within the school.

Knowing how to guide an interactive discussion is a spiritual gift. On the one hand, the facilitator should not manage the discussion in such a way that the participants feel they are being pushed toward some predetermined outcome or that their insights or creative interjections are not being valued. On the other hand, every group must be protected from participants who (often without realizing it) dominate discussions or tend to push the conversation off-track. The facilitator must also be able to recognize that some participants, by temperament, are more likely to speak up and express their views, while others tend to be more reflective and quiet and will not speak up unless they are prompted to do so. A good facilitator will know how to coax the quiet participants to give their input, while, at the same time, keeping the more aggressive participants from dominating the discussion. The key is to convey an irenic disposition, be gracious in all circumstances, and learn how to use affirmation appropriately. It is also vital that the facilitator make sure that the alumni/ae perspectives are heard and understood by all those gathered. The questions that should be posed to the alumni/ae and faculty will be determined largely by the narratives themselves, the overall chosen theme of the conversation, and the content of the book or article that may have been assigned as part of the project. The facilitator will have already prepared some focus questions to stimulate conversation.

If the event is part of a faculty retreat, then multiple sessions may be possible. If it takes place within the structure of the academic year and, therefore, takes place in the late afternoon or in the evening, it should not exceed an hour and a half. Furthermore, convey from the beginning the time frame of the event and keep to it. Another feature in effectively facilitating a guided conversation like this is to be able to determine quickly whether a statement being made is descriptive or prescriptive. Most of the time in these type of sessions, the statements will fall into one of these two categories. Keep a fairly firm distinction between the work of identifying or describing a problem or issue and that of naming what ought to be and prescribing a solution. Some people are generally better at diagnosing problems, while others are far better at proposing solutions once a problem has been identified. Some are, by nature, more optimistic and will always see the silver lining in every cloud. Others are more prone to see problems and will find the cloud in every silver lining. Some facilitators will want to openly acknowledge this in their opening remarks; others will be aware of these dynamics but may not mention them publicly. The facilitator should have large sheets of poster paper already in place and be able to distill what is being said into pithy summary statements.[18] It might be helpful to have several large sheets of paper that are used for listing different issues as they arise. For example, one list could describe the problems. A second list could propose solutions. A third list could identify larger trends that are influencing the church or society at large. These are just examples of ways to focus the conversation.

As a part of the planning for the overall structure of the event, it may be helpful (as a possible option) to have the venue for the guided conversation in one setting and then, after the conversation is over, transition to a shared meal or worship service. This approach will help to further communicate to the faculty that this activity is an institutional priority and that it should be taken seriously. Furthermore, even the simple transition to another setting can be a creative time for interaction and listening one to another.

Since developing more intentional kinds of assessment procedures is central to ATS accreditation today, it may be helpful to use this project as one part of an institution's strategy for doing a better job of assessment. The narrative approach is helpful because the narrative becomes the focus for faculty and alumni/ae interaction. Faculty are not forced into thinking that the alumni/ae are lecturing them on how to do a better job. Instead, faculty are being asked to help the alumni/ae respond to this issue and think through the issue together. However, in the process, the faculty should be challenged to think through how these themes may influence the work of ministerial preparation. This is why the follow-up to the alumni/ae meeting should be seen as an integral part of the project.

Guideline 8: Identification of Technical and Adaptive Problems

After the event, the academic dean, the facilitator, and, possibly, a few senior faculty members should meet and discuss what was learned. Two or three items should be chosen for a follow-up discussion, reflection, and specific action. Most of the items chosen will fall broadly into two groups of issues. One group of issues should be addressed (at least in part) by specific and identifiable changes. For example, the conversation may stimulate the need to discuss a needed educational policy change, a specific new course that needs to be offered, a change in the field education or mentored ministry program, or help in a hiring decision. The administration should not go into the session with any predetermined idea about what an ideal outcome might be. This approach will help foster more creativity and thoughtfulness in the discussion. Whatever arises and is identified should then be sent for consideration along with a request for some specific recommendation to the appropriate group(s). The second group of issues may require a more comprehensive response—a long-term, multifaceted strategy for institutional change.

These two types of problems have been helpfully identified by Ronald Heifetz and Donald Laurie as technical problems and adaptive problems (Heifetz and Laurie 1998, 172–197). Technical problems are problems with readily identifiable solutions within the institution, with mechanisms and expertise in place to identify and solve these problems. However, an institution must also be able to identify adaptive problems, which are problems that have no easy solution and require long-term strategic change to resolve. Technical problems can be solved by a leader who understands the problem and knows how to align the faculty to follow his or her vision in addressing a problem. Adaptive problems cannot be solved in this way. An adaptive problem involves mobilizing many people effectively around an issue and fostering long-term collaboration and adaptation to new realities. Frequently, administrators, as a part of their own managerial style and temperament, have the habit of reducing all problems to manageable technical problems that they think can be solved in one or two academic years. However, this kind of management style does not always help the institution to adapt or reposition itself over decades of time. Adaptive problems cannot be resolved in one or two years. Adaptive problems are, by definition, long-term strategic challenges. For example, what kind of response is required if it becomes clear in the guided discussions that many of the alumni/ae feel that they were simply ill prepared to minister within a context of ethnic diversity? The technical solution might be to add a new course on ministry in an ethnic context. This tactic may offer a good partial solution, but it can also mask a more fundamental, adaptive change that may be required for every single course in the institution.

In short, technical responses to adaptive problems can become a false panacea for the real transformation that is required. As painful as *curriculum* revision is, it is still a technical solution. *Faculty* revision, on the other hand, takes even longer, and is a fundamental, adaptive change. I am not referring only to the need to hire new or more diverse faculty (although this may be important), but rather transforming the way current faculty think about their discipline—adapting their pedagogy, changing the way they collaborate with other faculty, adjusting their attitudes, and thus empowering them to take initiative in areas that previously were not part of faculty life and ethos.

I am convinced that the alumni/ae Café Model conversation proposed here can be useful in stimulating technical and adaptive change based on what is learned from the alumni/ae about the nature of the ministries for which we teach.

Guideline 9: Structuring the Follow-up Retreat

This chapter has, among other things, highlighted the challenges of the dramatic growth of the church in the Majority World and the new realities of a post-Western Christianity. The shifting center of global Christianity is the most important adaptive challenge that the church in the West faces. Therefore, the four alumni/ae conversations should culminate in a retreat that focuses on the longer-term, adaptive changes needed in light of the dramatic megachanges in Christianity here and in the larger global context.

In this final phase of the project, each of the twelve alumni/ae are invited to return and participate with the faculty in a culminating retreat at a location away from the normal institutional setting. The alumni/ae should be joined by available members of the trustees so that, together with the faculty, significant discussions concerning major adaptive challenges can take place. The challenge of the shifting center of global Christianity is so complex and multifaceted that addressing it fully in the four alumni/ae visits and accompanying conversations is not possible. The more extended setting of a faculty retreat allows more time to explore what the shift in the center of Christian gravity means for the future of the institution. Reading Jenkins's *The Next Christendom* (2002) or *The New Faces of Christianity* (2006) or Lamin Sanneh's *Whose Religion Is Christianity?* (2003) and framing a discussion around the thesis of one of these books would be a good start. As in the earlier discussions, it is impossible to predict the possible outcomes. The responses may take many forms. However, even when facing massive, adaptive problems, it is important to find practical steps toward a long-term solution. For example, if the retreat reveals that the faculty are not sufficiently in touch with global changes, then perhaps creative ways could be explored to enable members of the faculty to be guest lecturers at seminaries around the world and, in turn, to host Majority World scholars to come and offer regular or intensive courses at their institution. It may be that these discussions might influence future faculty hiring or the kinds of courses that are needed. Developing a more robust atmosphere of cross-fertilization should be a helpful contribution toward a long-term strategy for the kind of adaptive change needed in twenty-first-century theological education.

At other institutions, it may be discovered that a number of the faculty have extensive experience around the world, but the administration has not found a way to tap into that resource so it can benefit the ethos and reflection of the larger faculty. A framework could be established that enables a faculty member who travels abroad to teach to reflect on this experience with the entire faculty.

To better address some of these issues, it may be helpful to frame the retreat discussions along the three questions developed by Craig Dykstra of the Lilly Endowment. First, what is God doing in the world? Second, what does the church need to be like in order to align itself with what God is doing in the world? Third, what does our seminary/divinity school need to be like if we are going to equip the church to align itself with what God is doing in the world (Mouw 2007; Dykstra 1999, 153)? Each area of the institution could be challenged to think about how these new global realities might influence their particular discipline. Three or four alumni/ae who are serving in cross-cultural contexts around the world could even be invited to log onto Skype or submit a short video whereby each of them is asked his or her perspective on the key questions noted above. This approach would almost certainly stimulate some excellent discussion and reflection.

A retreat cannot change an institution. However, one of the guiding values of this project is that if we can change the conversation, we can change the future. Ongoing, intentional discussions on this theme will, over time, give rise to a number of important technical changes that need to be implemented. More importantly, they will eventually give rise to long-term, adaptive changes in the life and ethos of the faculty and institution.

Conclusion

The Dutch missiologist Hendrick Kraemer once commented, "The church is always in a state of crisis, its greatest shortcoming is that it is only occasionally aware of it" (Bosch 1991, 2). What was said of the church can certainly also be said of seminaries and divinity schools. The focus of this chapter has been to shed light on the crisis and explore the growing disjuncture between what goes on in seminaries and divinity schools and what occurs in the actual ministries to which our students are called. Furthermore, this chapter has highlighted global developments within the broader Christian movement that will undoubtedly have a defining influence on the role and nature of theological education in the twenty-first century. It is hoped that these reflections, coupled with a specific model to assist administrators and faculties in thinking about these issues, will serve to strengthen and enrich our theological communities to creatively respond to the challenges that confront us today.

Appendix A

Narrative Guidelines[19]

The Assignment. Stories are powerful tools for individuals as well as churches. They reveal our values and assumptions; they shed light on our struggles and concerns; they depict the contours and consequences of our lives and ministries. Churches are communities with shared memories and collective imaginations. As such, they are brimming with stories. These stories are often filled with dilemmas and humor, tradition, and forces of change, chaos, and grace. We invite you to share a brief story about your church and ministry that gives some insight from your ministry and might help your alma mater be more effective in preparing men and women for ministry in today's changing contexts. Your assignment is to write a two-page narrative that tells a story in keeping with the suggested theme that you have been given by the dean's office. The story should capture and embody the challenges and opportunities that you are facing in your ministry.

The Form. A particular dilemma, a challenge, a need for change or some ministerial quandary you have faced may provide the best action points for the story you will be sharing. The tension may be between individuals or groups or with other kinds of values, traditions, or developments that you are facing. You may use a real event as a starting point in your mind, but the narrative should not be a transcription; rather, it is a fictionalized account and may be inspired by a single event or a composite of several events. Let your imagination fill in the details. The text should reflect the fluid language, diction, and dialogue of a story. Include a title that captures the story in some provocative or insightful way.

The Process. You are writing one narrative along with two other alumni/ ae who are also writing narratives. The three of you will all submit your own narratives to the dean's office, and all three will be distributed to the faculty and provide the basis for the discussion during your campus visit. Prior to your visit, you will receive copies of the other two narratives so that you will be familiar with all three of the stories that will be shared and discussed with the faculty. You have been invited to come on campus and participate in a conversational café with the faculty concerning various problems and challenges that you and others are facing. Someone from the dean's office will contact you with more of the details about the actual visit and the structure of the conversation with the faculty.

Notes

1. Craig Carter (2006) has pointed out, quite persuasively, that Richard Niebuhr's five classic categories relating Christ and culture are all expressed within a Christendom framework and are no longer adequate for Western Christians in the twenty-first century context.
2. Langdon Gilkey (1969), in his *Naming the Whirlwind*, carefully traces the way in which mainline Protestantism unsuccessfully tried to reconcile Christianity with modernist, antisupernaturalistic notions.
3. This fifteen-year period is typical of the larger trend over the entire twentieth century. In fact, during the twentieth century, the African church grew, on average, by 16,500 members every day, while the Western church lost between 4,000 and 7,500 members per day. The result is that although the African church began the twentieth century with fewer than 100 million members, it ended the century with over 367 million members (Isichei 1995).
4. These Christian movements around the world have produced a staggering array of new denominations. Currently, the *World Christian Encyclopedia* (Barrett, Kurian, and Johnson 2001) has documented 34,000 separate denominations in the world today.
5. For more on this global theological conversation, see Tennent (2007).
6. In 1995 Roland Robertson joined the words "global" and "local" to form the word "glocal" as a way of describing the need for theological education and ministerial training to be both local and global at the same time. See Robertson (1991).
7. Extensive documentation can be obtained from the Auburn Center for the Study of Theological Education (http://www.auburnsem.org) and from the statistical data published by ATS and available online in their *Fact Book on Theological Education* (www.ats.edu). See, especially, the analysis of the ATS member schools' student and faculty diversity by gender and ethnicity.
8. See, for example, the narrative, reflections, and project report of Virginia Theological Seminary (1999a, 1999b).
9. According to Barrett, Kurian, and Johnson (2001), there were 120,000 evangelicals in Spain in 2000, whereas Nepal had 185,000. By the year 2025 Spain is projected

to have 131,000 evangelicals compared with Nepal's 405,000. This figure does not count the 1.3 million Pentecostals in Nepal.

10. The assistant should become familiar with the narrative approach by going to The Lexington Seminar Web site (www.lexingtonseminar.org).

11. Note that the word "meeting" should be avoided, because of the negative associations that the word conveys to many of the faculty. In fact, as will become clear as the project unfolds, it may be helpful to use the phrase "café gatherings."

12. Skype is a software program that allows users to communicate through their computers free of charge. It not only enables high-quality conversations but also file transfers and instant messaging.

13. You may want to provide a few examples of books or writings that explore this concept from different perspectives, such as Wells, *Above All Earthly Powers: Christ in a Postmodern World* (2005); Stone, *Evangelism after Christendom* (2007); or Penner, *Christianity and the Postmodern Turn: Six Views* (2005).

14. Background reading might include Pozetta, *The Immigrant Religious Experience* (1991).

15. Background reading might include Anderson, *Spiritual Caregiving as Secular Sacrament: A Practical Theology for Professional Caregivers* (2003).

16. As noted earlier, deans who are using this project as a part of new ATS standards for assessment may want to focus the themes, using language consistent with ATS categories. Examples of narratives can be found on The Lexington Seminar Web site. See www.lexingtonseminar.org.

17. More specifics about this are explored later with the introduction of the World Café Model.

18. The dean's administrative assistant should purchase the large Post-it poster sheets rather than the traditional type. This allows them to be placed on a wall for all to see as each sheet is filled with ideas.

19. Adapted from the narrative guidelines used by The Lexington Seminar. See www.lexingtonseminar.org.

References

Anderson, Ray. 2003. *Spiritual Caregiving as Secular Sacrament: A Practical Theology for Professional Caregivers*. London: Jessica Kingsley Publishers.

Banks, Robert. 1999. *Reenvisioning Theological Education*. Grand Rapids: Eerdmans.

Barrett, David B., George T. Kurian, and Todd M. Johnson. 2001. *World Christian Encyclopedia*, 2nd ed. New York: Oxford University Press.

Bediako, Kwame. 1995. *Christianity in Africa*. Maryknoll, NY: Orbis Books.

Berger, Peter L. 1999. "The Desecularization of the World: A Global Overview." In *The Desecularization of the World: Resurgent Religion and World Politics*, ed. Peter L. Berger. Grand Rapids: Eerdmans.

Bonk, Jonathan. 2004. "Ecclesiastical Cartography and the Invisible Continent." *International Bulletin of Missionary Research* 28 (4): 153–158.

Bosch, David. 1991. *Transforming Mission*. Maryknoll, NY: Orbis Books.

Bowder, Bill. 2004. "Worship Numbers Fall Again." *Church Times*, Issue 7349, January 16. http://www.churchtimes.co.uk/content.asp?id=21258

Brown, Juanita, and David Isaacs. 2005. *The World Café: Shaping our Futures through Conversations That Matter*. San Francisco: Berrett-Koehler Publishers.

Calvin Theological Seminary. 1999. Project Narrative. http://www.lexingtonseminar. org/archive/archive_doc.php/doctype/narrative/id/260/

Carter, Craig A. 2006. *Rethinking Christ and Culture: A Post-Christendom Perspective.* Grand Rapids: Brazos Press, 2006.

Claremont School of Theology. 2000. Project Narrative. http://www.lexingtonseminar. org/archive/archive_doc.php/doctype/narrative/id/266/

Cox, Harvey. 1995. *Fire from Heaven: The Rise of Pentecostal Spirituality and the Reshaping of Religion in the 21st Century.* Reading, MA: Addison Wesley.

Dowson, Martin, and Dennis McInerney. 2005. "For What Should Theological Colleges Educate? A Systematic Investigation of Ministry Education Perceptions and Priorities." *Review of Religious Research* 46 (4): 403–421.

Dykstra, Craig. 1999. *Growing in the Life of Faith: Education and Christian Practices.* Louisville, KY: Geneva Press.

Eastern Baptist Theological Seminary. 2000. Project Narrative. http://www.lexington-seminar.org/archive/archive_doc.php/doctype/narrative/id/268/

Episcopal Theological Seminary of the Southwest. 2005. Project Narrative. http:// www.lexingtonseminar.org/archive/archive_doc.php/doctype/narrative/ id/368/

Escobar, Samuel. 2004. "What Is the Ministry toward Which We Teach?" In *Practical Wisdom: On Theological Teaching and Learning.* Ed. Malcolm L. Warford. New York: Peter Lang Publishing, Inc.

Gilkey, Langdon. 1969. *Naming the Whirlwind.* Indianapolis: Bobbs-Merrill Co.

Gledhill, Ruth. 2003. "Archbishop Thanks Africa for Lessons on Faith." *The Times* (London), July 26.

"Global Challenges and Perspectives in Theological Education." 1986. *Theological Education* 23 (1; autumn): 1–83.

"Globalizing Theological Education in North America." 1986. *Theological Education* 22 (2; spring): 1–137.

Harvard Divinity School. 2006. Project Narrative. http://www.lexingtonseminar.org/ archive/archive_doc.php/doctype/narrative/id/403/

Harvard Divinity School. 2006–2007. Catalog.

Heifetz, Ronald, and Donald Laurie. 1998. "The Work of Leadership." In *Harvard Business Review on Leadership.* Cambridge, MA: Harvard Business School Press.

Isichei, Elizabeth. 1995. *A History of Christianity in Africa.* Grand Rapids: Eerdmans.

Jenkins, Philip. 2002. *The Next Christendom: The Coming of Global Christianity.* New York: Oxford University Press.

———. 2006. *The New Faces of Christianity: Believing the Bible in the Global South.* New York: Oxford University Press.

Johnson, Todd M., and Sun Young Chung. 2004. "Tracking Global Christianity's Statistical Centre of Gravity, AD 33–AD 2100." *International Review of Mission* 93 (369): 166–181.

Kepel, Gilles. 1994. *The Revenge of God.* Cambridge, MA: Polity Press. Quoted in Harvey Cox. 1995. *Fire from Heaven: The Rise of Pentecostal Spirituality and the Reshaping of Religion in the 21st Century.* Reading, MA: Addison Wesley, xvii.

Kierkegaard, Søren. 1968. *Attack upon Christendom.* Trans. Walter Lowrie. Princeton, NJ: Princeton University Press.

Kinnaman, David, and Gabe Lyons. 2007. *UnChristian: What a New Generation Really Thinks about Christianity—and Why It Matters.* Grand Rapids: Baker Academic.

Klimoski, Victor J., Kevin J. O'Neil, and Katarina M. Schuth. 2005. "Diversity and the Formation for Ministry." In *Educating Leaders for Ministry: Issues and Responses*. Collegeville, MN: Liturgical Press.

Knippers, Dianne. 2003. "The Anglican Mainstream: It's Not Where Americans Might Think," *Weekly Standard*, August 25.

Leithart, Peter J. 2008. *Solomon among the Postmoderns*. Grand Rapids: Brazos Press.

Lexington Theological Seminary. 2002. Project Narrative. http://www.lexingtonseminar.org/archive/archive_doc.php/doctype/narrative/id/279/

Lutheran Theological Seminary at Gettysburg. 2003. Project Narrative. http://www.lexingtonseminar.org/archive/archive_doc.php/doctype/narrative/id/291/

Lyotard, Jean-Francois. 1985. *The Postmodern Condition: A Report on Knowledge*. Minneapolis: University of Minnesota Press.

Mbiti, John S. 1976. "Theological Impotence and the Universality of the Church." In *Mission Trends No. 3: Third World Theologies*, ed. Gerald H. Anderson and Thomas F. Stransky. New York: Paulist Press; Grand Rapids: Eerdmans.

MIT. 2007. MITOpenCourseware. http://ocw.mit.edu/OcwWeb/web/about/history/index.htm.

Mouw, Richard J. 2007. Interview by Jay Blossom. *In Trust Magazine* (summer). www.intrust.org/magazine/article_print.cfm?id=512&CFID=905&CFTOKEN=43%951339.

Neill, Stephen. 1952. *The Christian Society*. London: Collins. Quoted in Kwame Bediako. 2005. *Christianity in Africa*. Maryknoll, NY: Orbis Books, 205.

Penner, Myron B., ed. 2005. *Christianity and the Postmodern Turn: Six Views*. Grand Rapids: Brazos Press.

Pozetta, George E. 1991. *The Immigrant Religious Experience*. London: Taylor and Francis.

Robert, Dana. 2000. "Shifting Southward: Global Christianity since 1945." *International Bulletin of Missionary Research* 24 (2): 50–58.

Robertson, Roland. 1991. "Globalization, Modernization, and Postmodernization: The Ambiguous Position of Religion." In *Religion and Global Order*, ed. Roland Robertson and William Garrett, 281–291. New York: Paragon.

Sanneh, Lamin. 2003. *Whose Religion Is Christianity? The Gospel Beyond the West*. Grand Rapids: Eerdmans.

Schuller, David. 1993. "Globalization: Tracing the Journey, Charting the Course." *Theological Education* 30 (supplement 1): 1–13.

Shriver, Donald W., Jr. 1986. "The Globalization of Theological Education: Setting the Task." *Theological Education* 22 (2): 7–18.

Stone, Bryan. 2007. *Evangelism after Christendom*. Grand Rapids: Baker Academic.

Tennent, Timothy. 2007. *Theology in the Context of Global Christianity: How the Global Church Is Helping Us to Think about and Discuss Theology*. Grand Rapids: Zondervan.

Tertullian, *De Praescriptione Haereticorum* 7.9.

Tiénou, Tite. 2007. Interview by Timothy C. Tennent. February 8. Deerfield, IL.

Tomlinson, John. 1999. *Globalization and Culture*. Chicago: University of Chicago Press.

Tracy, David. 1998. "Traditions of Spiritual Practice and the Practice of Theology." *Theology Today* 55 (2): 235–239.

Trinity Evangelical Divinity School. 2003. Project Narrative. http://www.lexingtonseminar.org/archive/archive_doc.php/doctype/narrative/id/295/

Virginia Theological Seminary. 1999a. Project Narrative. http://www.lexingtonseminar. org/archive/archive_doc.php/doctype/narrative/id/263/

————. 1999b. Project Report. http://www.lexingtonseminar.org/archive/archive_doc. php/doctype/report/id/263/

Walls, Andrew. 1996. *The Missionary Movement in Christian History: Studies in the Transmission of Faith*. Maryknoll, NY: Orbis Press.

Wells, David. 2005. *Above All Earthly Powers: Christ in a Postmodern World*. Grand Rapids: Eerdmans.

Schools Participating in The Lexington Seminar

1999

Austin Presbyterian Theological Seminary
Calvin Theological Seminary
Lutheran School of Theology at Chicago
Regent College
Virginia Theological Seminary

2000

Associated Mennonite Theological Seminary
Claremont School of Theology
Eastern Baptist (*now* Palmer) Theological Seminary
McCormick Theological Seminary
Seabury-Western Theological Seminary

2001

Bethel Theological Seminary
Church Divinity School of the Pacific
Luther Seminary
Pacific Lutheran Theological Seminary
United Theological Seminary of the Twin Cities

2002

Colgate Rochester Crozer Divinity School
General Theological Seminary
Gordon-Conwell Theological Seminary
Lexington Theological Seminary
Lutheran Theological Seminary at Philadelphia

2003

Lutheran Theological Seminary at Gettysburg
Methodist Theological School in Ohio
Phillips Theological Seminary
Pittsburgh Theological Seminary
Trinity Evangelical Divinity School

2004

Ashland Theological Seminary
Baptist Theological Seminary at Richmond
Lancaster Theological Seminary
Lutheran Theological Southern Seminary
Wesley Theological Seminary

2005

Bethany Theological Seminary
Eastern Mennonite Seminary
Episcopal Theological Seminary of the Southwest
Trinity Lutheran Seminary
Wartburg Theological Seminary

2006

Candler School of Theology, Emory University
Harvard Divinity School
University of Notre Dame Department of Theology
Vanderbilt Divinity School

2007

Duke Divinity School
Emmanuel College, University of Toronto
Princeton Theological Seminary
Union Theological Seminary
Yale Divinity School

Contributors

JOSEPH A. BESSLER is the Robert Travis Peake Associate Professor of Theology at Phillips Theological Seminary, Tulsa, Oklahoma.

PETER T. CHA is Associate Professor of Pastoral Theology at Trinity Evangelical Divinity School, Deerfield, Illinois.

MARY E. HESS is Associate Professor of Educational Leadership at Luther Seminary, St. Paul, Minnesota.

TIMOTHY C. TENNENT is Professor of World Missions and Indian Studies at Gordon-Conwell Theological Seminary, South Hamilton, Massachusetts.

MALCOLM L. WARFORD is Director of The Lexington Seminar: Theological Teaching for the Church's Ministries and Research Professor, Lexington Theological Seminary, Lexington, Kentucky.

Index

fueling secularizing impulse, 3–4
Educating Clergy (Foster et al.), 36, 49
education, integration-oriented
    approach to, 39–40
efficiency, limits on improving, 12
endowments, range in size of, 6,
    28–29n13
Enlightenment, growing reaction
    against, in West, 101
Escobar, Samuel, 99–100
evangelical movement, institutional and
    educational strategies of, 4–5

faculty
    allegiance of, 25
    avoiding split in, between
        commitments to academic vision
        and ministry, 26
    challenges facing, when addressing
        student preparation, 72
    creative tension of, between personal
        and seminary's vocations,
        26–27
    development models for, 15–26,
        114–29
    differing backgrounds from
        students, 68–69
    discomfort of, with the social
        sciences, 119
    encouraging to listen deeply, 73–79
    goals of, 69
    identity of, new paradigm for, 12–15
    learning art of collaboration, 76
    learning to be more collaborative
        teachers, 109–10
    learning to profess faith in
        educational context, 79–81
    at margins of congregational life, 25
    mismatch between preparation of,
        and actual tasks, 67, 68
    as obstacle to adaptive change, 8–10
    outreach to constituents, 13
    pressures facing, 75–76
    redesigning advisor-advisee
        relationship for, 41–42
    reexamining thinking about training
        and the ministry, 109
    seeing challenges with realism and
        hope, 20–21

understanding students' relationship
    with a subject, 71–72
visualizing ministerial
    settings, 122–23
faith
    communities of, 69
    professing and confessing,
        in educational context,
        79–81
Farley, Edward, 9, 11
fiscal resources, of seminaries and
    divinity schools, viii–ix
formation, 44–45
    curriculum goals for, 77–78
    differing definitions for, 63n2
    diversity in, among M.Div.
        students, 35–36
    growing emphasis on, 36
    incorporating concern for students'
        well-being, 45–48
    pastoral model of, 45–48
formation by osmosis, 35
forum theater groups, 55
Foster, Charles, 36

*Gifts of the Muse: Reframing the Debate
    about the Benefits of the Arts*
    (McCarthy et al.), 18
Gilkey, Langdon, 131n2
global consciousness, teaching and
    learning with, 104–106
globalization, 100–101, 107–108
Gordon, A. J., 105
Gordon-Conwell Theological
    Seminary, 74–75, 105, 110, 112
Gordon Divinity School, 105
gospel, as one message among
    many, 100
Gottlieb, Adolph, vii
grand narratives, collapse of, 101
group dynamics, improvisational
    sculpting of, 61–62

habitat, renewal of, 15
Handbook of Accreditation (ATS), 18
Harvard Divinity School, 78,
    104–105, 108–12
Heifetz, Ronald, 2, 12, 127
Hess, Mary, 54